W9-BCB-882

6737

DAVID BOOTH

Censorship Goes to School

Pembroke Publishers Limited

YORK COLLEGE
PENNSYLVANIA

LIBRARY

© 1992 David Booth

Pembroke Publishers
538 Hood Road
Markham, Ontario
L3R 3K9

All rights reserved.
No part of this publication may be reproduced in any form or by any means electronic or mechanical, including photocopy, recording, or any information or retrieval system, without permission in writing from the publisher.

Canadian Cataloguing in Publication Data

Booth, David W. (David Wallace)
  Censorship goes to school

Includes bibliographical references.
ISBN 0-921217-87-0

1. English literature – Study and teaching
(Elementary). 2. English literature – Study and
teaching (Secondary). 3. English literature –
Censorship. 4. English literature – Curricula.
I. Title.

LB1575.B66 1992   372.64   C92-094765-4

Editor: David Kilgour
Design: John Zehethofer
Cover Photography: Ajay Photographics
Typesetting: Jay Tee Graphics Ltd.

This book was produced with the generous assistance of the government of Ontario through the Ministry of Culture and Communications.

Printed and bound in Canada by Webcom
9 8 7 6 5 4 3 2 1

Contents

Introduction

Book banning goes back a long way for me.

My great-grandmother was a slave in Charleston, South Carolina; she was bought and sold there. It was against the law, after slavery, for all Black people to learn to read and write. During slavery you could have your ears, or your nose, or even your life cut off, because knowledge was considered a very dangerous thing. For a person in bondage to be able to read and write meant that revolt would be on the way. . .

Then, with freedom there came another kind of banning. As it became legal for Blacks to learn to read and write, school boards without Black members selected all the reading matter; even all-Black schools were not allowed to select their own books. Of course, reading material for Blacks was already banned in another way; the public libraries of South Carolina and of other Jim Crow states were closed to my people. We were not allowed to withdraw books.

Alice Childress,
On Censorship

Censorship has always been a delicate issue for parents and educators alike: which books do we thrust on our children, which ones do we hide, which ones — if any — do we forbid them to read? At home, as parents, we can control, more or less, the books our children have access to, but in our schools and libraries we have a more complex situation, and this troubles some parents.

In recent years, our method of teaching children to read has been changing rapidly. Gone are the days of the controlled vocabulary readers of Dick and Jane. In their place children find anthologies of traditional and contemporary writers, alongside picture books, novels, and folktales written by authentic authors with something to say. At a time when many parents feel battered by the tensions and pressures of the changing and difficult world their children live in, censoring what they read may appear a simple and powerful way of maintaining control over their fragile lives, and a number of parents have advocated that some books be removed from schools and libraries. The reach of book banners affects many facets of education in today's schools.

I am no stranger to censorship. During my first year of teaching, thirty-five years ago, the teachers at my school received a memo requesting us to come in at 9:00 a.m. on a Saturday morning to tear out from each of the grade four readers a story about Brer Rabbit. A black parent had objected to the origins of this tale in the stereotypical "Uncle Remus" folkloric stories of plantation life in the American south. Dutifully, several of us arrived at the school, carefully cut out all the copies of the story, destroyed them, and then returned the books to the children's desks. I'm not sure if the children or their parents were any the wiser, but as teachers we felt very strange working in secret to remove a story that had been around for so long. How interesting to find last year the Uncle Remus tales reprinted in a lovely new version — and reviewed positively in the press!

As a high school language arts consultant, I was once called to my superintendent's office, where he shared with me a complaint he'd had from a parent about a novel used in the school, a rather innocuous book in retrospect. A conservative man, the superintendent was deeply concerned, sensing confrontation in the wind. I explained that I had read the book and there was nothing in it that should cause difficulty, but that the school had many other books, and perhaps the child of the complaining parent could choose another selection. The superintendent then revealed to me his own solution: "David, what we need for our students are more books about bears. I mean, bears are so Canadian, and they don't cause anybody any trouble." The irony was that I had just read Marian Engel's *Bear*, in which the creature of the title and the female protagonist have a rather intense love affair. I suppose the superintendent did not recognize that even in remote wilderness communities life went on, with all the many problems that face adults and children.

In the early '70s, when screen education had become a part

of the curriculum in secondary school, I co-authored a book called *Film*. We used shots from movies, reviews, articles, commentary, and criticism as a base for helping young people study movies as a contemporary phenomenon of learning. One of the photographs was from a contemporary Alan King movie, a documentary about a Canadian family. In the still, a naked baby was pictured sitting between its parents. I was called to a school by a principal who accused me of shameful misconduct for portraying nudity in books for children — even though his school, being K-8, would never have used the book. However, he had seen it at a display. His red face and trembling voice betrayed his deep angst over the fact that a male child under one should be seen unclothed. It was the only complaint I heard about that book, and the publisher forwarded no others to me.

In the literature anthologies I first co-edited, a series called *Colours*, we included a ballad that was the cause of the only letter we received advocating censorship. In the ballad, the villain wielded a pen knife and a principal objected to the use of that word for fear children would gather pen knives and stab each other. So far, no woundings have been reported as a result of reading those books.

My most personal experience of censorship happened more recently. In the last five years I have had calls from Tom Brokaw's producer, Geraldo's story editor, the editor from the *New York Times*, a reporter from the *Times* of London, a producer from "Good Morning America", and an interviewer from CBC's "Fifth Estate", all wanting to interview me about the scandal concerning the challenges to a series of "whole language" readers called *Impressions*, which I co-edited. In the battle to save the series from censors, I have endured years of anguish and reflection; the result is this book, an attempt to understand the furor.

I read all the material I could get my hands on in researching the book, and I was both gladdened and depressed by my findings. In my own self-absorption, I had thought that *Impressions* was the only series of texts challenged, but on reading account after account, I recognized the scale of the problem of deciding what children read in school, and I felt like a member of some giant international seminar struggling to develop an action plan that would respect parents, enrich children, and support teachers. James Moffett's book *Storm in the Mountains* strengthened me at every turn, and I acknowledge my debt to his clarity of thought and compassion for others with different views.

But it was my son who gave me my philosophy of using books in school. Watching him develop as a reader, as he went through the books we chose together, talked and wondered about the issues and the characters that filled the pages, built his world view from the various authors who somehow spoke to him, altered me and gave me renewed respect for writers for children. I need them — even when I don't like them or agree with the views expressed by them — to extend and enrich my son's world, to continue what I began, to illuminate those of life's universal truths which I have — wittingly or otherwise — left in the shadows, hidden or glossed over. I have no fear of books for him.

I hope that my book can in a small way help start a constructive debate among those of us concerned with children's lives, to understand the complexities of the issues, so that we can work toward a policy about books that involves the whole community in building a school curriculum, mindful of the needs of each of those involved, and respectful of what is worked out through discussion, negotiation, and support of a given community's decisions. Because I want it to be a true debate I have tried to let as many voices speak for themselves — even if I do allow myself the last word.

In reading great literature I become a thousand men and yet remain myself. Like a night sky in the Greek poem, I see with a myriad eyes, but it is still I who see. Here, as in worship, in love, in moral action, and in knowing, I transcend myself; and am never more myself than when I do.

C.S. Lewis,
An Experiment in Criticism

1. Censorship and Children's Books

Censorship versus Selection

Is there a difference between censorship and selection? Censorship has been defined as the removal, suppression, or restricted circulation of literary, artistic, or educational images, ideas, and/or information on the grounds that they are morally or otherwise objectionable.

On the other hand, advocates of book selection argue that we must have standards for literary quality, and a knowledge of child development, in order to make decisions about choosing and using children's books, both at home and in school. According to this view, the application of the guidelines of selection is left to individual parents and professionals. Contrary to the arguments of many would-be censors, advocates of selection do not argue that all books are equally appropriate for children of all ages, and they understand that children are influenced by what they read. Selection operates according to a set of standards agreed upon by a group that looks at all the literature available to parents and children and makes choices based on a positive attitude to quality reading — even when that reading reveals unpleasant truths or viewpoints opposed to those of a particular parent or child, as long as the child is deemed capable of dealing with such ideas.

By purging schools and libraries of certain "controversial" books, by circulating lists of "objectionable" books and authors, censors hope to make decisions for others, to limit access. They believe that everyone should be coerced into thinking as they do. How can those of us who favor selection support a wide variety of options, respect individual differences, and agree to disagree?

Before 1960 there was a general consensus about children's literature; difficult, taboo topics such as death, racial conflict, or sexual permissiveness simply didn't appear in stories for children. However, the changes of the '60s and '70s altered children's books forever. A new kind of children's book came along, dealing with all sorts of sensitive issues. By the late 1970s, many books had come under attack from parents demanding that the books be banned in both school and public libraries. In the '90s the trend shows no sign of abating; censorship has become a major force in both the writing and the publishing of children's literature, and in the selection of school texts.

It is a complicated issue. Who should decide what our children read? This is a debate about freedom of expression, with one side holding beliefs about childhood different from the other's, one side claiming that some books are "immoral", the other claiming that free speech is a fundamental ideal of our society. Many of the important issues our children will read about involve difficult and disturbing ideas. How we deal with book choice may determine the future of public education. Because most children are enrolled in public schools, the books we use may be part of the creation of a sense of common culture and common heritage.

How will schools and libraries fight the "chill" factor, not selecting certain books because they know of the challenges from some groups that may lie ahead? Will they censor themselves? Many librarians have seen instances where an angry reader has whited out or inked out offensive portions of a book, or torn out a controversial page. Maurice Sendak's *Mickey in the Night Kitchen* features a nude child whose genitals, in many copies, have been obliterated by school officials and librarians themselves.

As for those of us responsible for helping children choose textbooks and library books, we must be very professional in determining our criteria for selecting books, and use research to support our choices. We must recognize our own biases and struggle to know what books we must fight for. We must include in our "support files" — a current necessity for educators everywhere — policy statements, useful resources, and guidelines from recognized authorities. We must communicate with parents constantly through open discussion about children's books, helping parents to understand why we choose specific titles in the first place. We must develop school policy statements dealing with censorship issues and we must understand procedures for formal complaints in order to cope with attempts to censor specific books.

Censorship runs against the basic values of our pluralist culture, and yet a growing number of school boards have faced pressure from citizens' groups to ban books. While the protests may seem amusing or trivial to others, they appear less so to the objects of the attacks. When friends and colleagues simply laughed at the "nuisance" of the attacks on my books, I became aware of two significant problems: Canadian educators have seldom before taken advocates of censorship seriously, and they have given even less consideration to the reasons for attacks on books. When a parent or group of parents made a complaint, often a school board banned the book in question without a trial, without bothering with details such as charges and examination of the facts. The removal of a book effectively endorsed the view that it was guilty of some offence.

There will always be different points of view about appropriate instructional material and textbooks for use in schools. However, fair and open procedures of selection will help avoid extreme positions, and if a system is in place for handling attempts at censorship, those policies will assist the sides involved in coming to some kind of settlement. We must stand against censorship while respecting the opinions of the complainants.

We must also refuse to be bullied by scare tactics. Often, through skilful manipulation, public rallies, and media campaigns, censors may appear to have a majority of the community's support. But we who are challenged must mobilize the support of the silent majority and encourage discussion and debate. The broader the base of the coalition in which parents, professional associations, and advocate groups can work together, the better the chance for community support in school decisions. While censors typically present their challenges as tests of religious faith, the policy educational authorities follow must concern those values common to all.

I do feel there is a difference between selection and censorship, between choosing books to put in our classrooms and burning books in the playground. When we act professionally and carefully select stories intended to help our children become readers, we are building a standard for literary excellence. None of us who advocate selection want to bypass the normal procedures of our society for developing curriculum and learning materials. We recognize the guidelines and processes adhered to by our school boards and officials. Why is it, then, that censors so often want to bypass these procedures and use frightening tactics to do away with books or even whole courses? Why do they want to withhold information, or to restrict knowledge, so that we cannot be informed citizens making proper choices? Why do censors often not look at a book as a whole but fasten on a single aspect — a word, a paragraph, an idea? Why do they so often refuse to read an entire book but rather concentrate on one objectionable feature?

Censorship afflicts every part of the country, from the metropolitan areas to the most remote communities. Censors are no longer targeting individual books but whole curricula. By moving censorship from the classrooms to the courtrooms, a group of American censors known as the "religious right" hope to win district court cases in order to give their doctrines official sanction. The recent history of the censorship movement coincides with major changes in school curricula. As they began to change, critics protested that new techniques of teaching reading would damage children, even destroy patriotism. And as the costs of education rose, some concerned parents called for a back-to-the-basics movement. One of their rallying cries was the control of books that they felt to be anti-God or anti-authority. Although I disagree with these parents, it must be said that they are not, as sometimes portrayed in the media, lunatics; they care as much about their children's welfare as we who oppose them do. But how can we balance the child's right to read, the teacher's right to teach, and the parent's right to choose an education for their children?

Of course, parents have the right to challenge what we are doing in schools, to complain, to air their views, but what will we do when their actions encroach upon the rights of other children to know and to read? Will parents take the time to read books under attack, to talk to others about courses and objectives, and to attend parent-teacher meetings?

As for educators, we must explain our programs to parents in terms they can understand, accept their concerns, their fears over controversial curricula, work with parent representatives on all-curriculum committees. We must not be afraid of working alongside parents, including those with deep political or religious convictions we do not share. Together we must forge a curriculum that will allow children freedom to read, freedom to think, and freedom to challenge and make their own decisions as lifelong learners.

At the same time, schools do have a compelling and legitimate interest in making a core curriculum mandatory. Educational goals in a democratic country such as ours require that students be prepared for full, responsible citizenship in a pluralist society. I believe that such citizenship requires the ability to think critically, to understand contradictions, to respect differing points of view, and to confront realities one finds objectionable. It is the unique obligation of educators to promote tolerance and a spirit of inquiry. Today schools present students with materials from real literature — materials that do not shelter them from life, or present a filtered, sugar-coated view of the world. If schools accede to every parent's demand to edit school materials and to remove all that they find improper, fearful, or objectionable, the result will be dangerously uninspiring books and a distorted view of society. And yet, as responsible citizens, students must learn to confront many difficult issues to build a world picture, as well as sharpen their own set of values.

According to Statistics Canada, only sixty-two percent of Canadian adults can read everyday materials such as newspapers, magazines, and books. A further twenty-two percent can read material that has a familiar context and is simply laid out. The remaining sixteen percent of Canadians aged sixteen to sixty-nine cannot read well enough to deal with the majority of printed material they encounter in everyday life. But fully ninety-four percent of adults feel their English or French reading skills are adequate for their daily activities. Are they right?

I'm most concerned about the forms of censorship that never make the headlines. I recently met a teacher, for example, who wants to teach *The Chocolate War*, but the department head is afraid that the book would cause trouble and won't order it. The book, in other words, wasn't thrown out of the classroom; it was simply prevented from ever entering it. This kind of quiet censorship is going on all of the time.

Then there is the censorship that goes on before books are even published. I know an author whose book wasn't picked up in paperback because of some controversy surrounding it. "From now," he says, "I'm writing squeaky clean books." It's terrible when authors start to feel they are under this kind of pressure. It's a form of censorship that nobody talks about, but it's happening all too often. I feel that this is the worst kind of censorship because it aborts ideas and stifles the creative act.

Robert Cormier (author of *The Chocolate War*),
Trust Your Children

Censorship is not only a contemporary concern. Between 1778 and 1789 Sarah Trimmer produced *The Family Magazine* for the "instruction and amusement of cottagers and servants". Here, as in her later writing, she hoped "to counteract the pernicious influence of immoral books" such as *Robinson Crusoe* and Perrault's fairy tales.

Formerly children's reading, whether for instruction or amusement, was confined to a very small number of volumes; of late years they have multiplied to an astonishing and alarming degree, and much mischief lies hid in many of them. The utmost circumspection is therefore requisite in making a proper selection; and children should not be permitted to make their own choice, or to read any books that may accidentally be thrown in their way, or offered to their perusal; but should be taught to consider it as a duty, to consult their parents in this momentous concern.

Novels certainly, however abridged, and however excellent, should not be read by young persons, till they are in some measure acquainted with real life; but under this denomination we do not mean to include those exemplary tales which inculcate the duties of childhood and youth without working too powerfully upon the feelings of the mind, or giving false pictures of life and manners.

Before we quit the subject of Books for Children, we must not omit to give a caution respecting those which go under the general name of School Books, viz. Grammars, Dictionaries, Spelling Books, Exercise Books, and Books of Geography, &c. into some of which the leaven of false philosophy has found its way. In short, there is not a species of Books for Children and Youth, any more than for those of maturer years, which has not been made in some way or other an engine of mischief; nay, even well-intentioned authors have, under a mistaken idea that it is necessary to conform to the taste of the times, contributed to increase the evil. However, there are in the mixed multitude, books of all sorts that are truly estimable; and others that might be rendered so with a little trouble in revising them; a task which we assure ourselves, the respective authors of these last-mentioned books will cheerfully undertake, for new Editions, if they consider the infinite importance it is of, to be correct in principle, and cautious in expression, when they are writing for the young and ignorant, upon whose minds new ideas frequently make very strong impressions.

Sarah Trimmer,
On the Care Which Is Requisite in the Choice of Books for Children (1803)

Trimmer did not advocate violence; more recent censors have. James Moffett's language arts series, published in the '70s, was the object of a violent attack in West Virginia, resulting in his innovative program disappearing from view.

In 1974 fundamentalists in Kanawha County, West Virginia, the area around Charleston, attacked several language arts programs just adopted by the district there. I had directed a new K-12 program for Houghton Mifflin called *Interaction* (1973). The school board had ignored the feelings of these people of the Appalachian culture, who were living mostly in outlying hills and hollows, until the wife of a fundamentalist preacher was elected to the board. Fresh from defeating a proposed sex education program, she challenged the adoptions in the spring and mobilized resistance over the summer. When school opened in September, the book protestors boycotted schools, picketed business, staged demonstrations, and persuaded the miners to strike. Thrown into consternation by these tough activist tactics, the board withdrew the books from schools while a citizen committee it appointed could assess them.

Meanwhile, school buses were shot at returning from their rounds; two men were wounded by gunfire at picket points; a television crew was roughed up; two elementary schools were firebombed at night; and the school board building itself was blasted by dynamite. Three fundamentalist ministers who had become leaders of the revolt were jailed for defying court injunctions, and one was ultimately sentenced to three years in prison for conspiracy in one of the school bombings. At one point in the fall everyone seemed so endangered that the superintendent cancelled all school events and ordered a four-day weekend, during which he and all the board members slipped out of town, including the woman who began it all. At the citizen committee's recommendation, the board sent back to classrooms in November all the books except one series and the senior high portion of Interaction. But further tumultuous controversy kept the county in disarray most of that school year and the superintendent and head of the board both resigned.

James Moffett,
Journal of Educational Thought, Vol. 24, No. 3A, December 1990

Censorship goes beyond schools and children's books. Perhaps the most publicized case in recent years is that of Salman Rushdie, who has had to remain in hiding for fear of his own life after the Ayatollah Khomeini put a bounty of $5.2 million on his head for publishing *The Satanic Verses*, a novel thought by some Muslims to be blasphemous.

Real Books for Real Children

Today, authentic literature — stories written by authors with a general audience in mind, rather than people producing textbooks aimed exclusively at students — is seen as leading children to a knowledge of the past, a love of language, a critical and creative approach to considering the world of others, and the hope they will continue to read as adults. Some difficulty lies in bringing these stories to the classroom, since authors have always represented the complex society in which they write, a society that is full of contradictions and problems. Often children are their protagonists, expressing their emotions and reactions through playfulness, teasing, jealousy, or anger. How characters deal with these feelings is sometimes the theme of stories. One of the fears that censoring parents have is that their children will "act out" some of the negative behaviors they read about in books. This fear is based on the false belief that somehow children would never have had those thoughts if they hadn't read the offending books.

It is true that the lives of children are changing drastically in today's world, and these developments are reflected in both the content of what they read and in their attitudes toward the act of reading. Family patterns are changing. Young people are becoming critical of adults in authority, and of siblings. They depend more and more on peer groups, their models are drawn more and more from entertainment stars, sports heroes, and books. They demand independence, testing their own positions at every stage. Literature may provide insights, giving young people roles for identification, situations for reflection, and opportunities for examining issues. Authors sometimes tackle complex topics through realistic settings, fantasy, science fiction, and mystery. Poetry gives young readers sensitive glimpses into all aspects of life and presents intimate pictures of personal experience. Special interest stories offer readers information about hobbies, social problems, world affairs, sports, and heroes.

The lives of some children are very full of friends, homework, sports, lessons, and chores. Reading may find itself squeezed out of the timetable. However, school success is greatly determined by literacy, and adults must help their children find time for books, give assistance in selecting books, and especially support those readers who are as yet not fluent or independent. Today's children's authors are writing stories that are interesting enough to keep children reading, yet with a reading range that enables young readers of different abilities to read successfully. Authors who have talent as well as the needs of the youngsters in mind create novels which, with continued help from adults, will give children a chance to become literate young people who want to read well.

Literature must cause children to think about and explore a wide variety of aspects of their world. Through suggestions and activities that accompany stories, teachers can facilitate discussions that allow children to grapple with the diversity of their own and others' cultures.

Significant literature is open to different responses and interpretations. A story perceived by one reader to have a "negative" emphasis may be perceived by another reader as having a "positive" emphasis. An example might be the story *A Taste of Blackberries* by Doris Buchanan Smith, in which a character dies from an allergic reaction to a bee sting.

The main character in the story reflects on his relationship with the victim, and wonders "who would we have to make us laugh now". The story holds tremendous possibilities for dealing with essential issues of how we treat each other (the victim was considered something of a pest and a show-off by others) and the value of all human life, as well as other topics such as allergies and people with unique physical needs. Do we define this as a "negative" statement of gloom and hopelessness or as a "positive" opportunity to discuss important issues and concerns?

Fiction for children revolves around several recurring themes — friends, family, dreams, humor, mystery, adventure, history, nature, and contemporary issues (all, by the way, dealt with in the Bible). Censors often have trouble with realistic novels that deal in the immediate, the "here-and-now" effects of specific actions and their consequences. Such novels present issues of behavior and ethics as they affect people in situations with which readers can identify. Common themes include parent-child relationships, friendships, sex roles, and social attitudes and values. A strong sense of where and how characters live can be created by careful attention to details of surroundings.

Realistic stories for children are generally optimistic, even if the characters are poor or have fallen on bad times. Books of this kind are not meant to be tragic, but are unromantic, honest portrayals of people who might really exist. Youngsters have common interests that are revealed in their reading choices; recurring themes reflect their developing lives and their questions about their place in society. While the context of a given story may be fantastical, the issues are real, and the problems faced are similar to those of many young readers. The analogies and the metaphors used by the authors of such fiction allow readers safe mirrors in which to examine their concerns. A fictional treatment of a problem with which the reader can identify allows him or her to see it from different viewpoints and to see how someone else might deal with it. The central issue in this type of story must be presented in a way that makes it universal and understandable to a wide range of people.

"Problem" stories are often left unresolved in order to stimulate readers to think about the story and to reach their own conclusions. The dilemma may be dealt with in such ways that readers gain insights into the way people think and act, and even, perhaps, into their own private selves. But no matter how difficult the subject matter they deal with, the philosophy of most children's writers is overwhelmingly positive, as witnessed by one of North America's most brilliant authors for children:

> When I write realistic novels, I will be true as best I am able to what is. But I am, as Zechariah says, a prisoner of hope. My stories will lean toward hope as a sunflower toward the sun. The roots will be firmly in the world as I know it, but the face will turn inevitably toward the peaceable kingdom, the heavenly city, the loving parent watching and waiting for the prodigal's return. Because, by the grace of God, that is truth for me and all who share this hope.
>
> Katherine Paterson,
> *The Spying Heart*

In 1982, Phyllis Schlafly's Eagle Forum lobbied successfully to eliminate required reading lists from the English curriculum of a high school in St. David, Arizona. The titles banned included *Of Mice and Men, Lord of the Flies*, and classics by Homer, Edgar Allan Poe, Nathaniel Hawthorne, Robert Louis Stevenson, and Ernest Hemingway. The contracts of teachers who spoke out against the censorship were not renewed.

It is easy to laugh at such extremism, but the fact is that during Ronald Reagan's first term as president of the U.S., attempts at censorship in that country increased by five times. In a publication by the joint commission of the Association of Supervision and Curriculum Development, and the American Library Association (1983), a five-year study on censorship in classrooms and libraries revealed that only about fifteen percent of the cases of library censorship uncovered by the study were reported in the media, that twice as many challenges came from organized groups as from individuals, and, surprisingly, that about a third of the original complaints came from members of the faculty or staff. In other words, attempts at censorship are not merely isolated incidents: they are initiated by many different interest groups at different levels.

Censoring School Texts

Many books read by students in schools have been accused of being anti-family, anti-country, or against traditional values. For example, if children help their parents solve problems in a story, some critics feel the author may be undermining parental authority. Some censors may feel that stories portray women too traditionally, while others argue that books should be banned because they describe too many career women. Who's right?

Textbook publishers are particularly susceptible to censorship because of the economics of the publishing industry. Textbook publishers sell only to school systems. If a major school system refuses to buy a certain textbook unless the publisher makes changes, the publisher is often forced by economic necessity to make changes.

As well, children have almost no choice in using or not using a required text. Is it possible to create school books of any value if every interest group has a say in what is to be included?

Textbooks are certainly complicated educational tools. Some educators complain that they represent a form of cultural domination, that they stress out-of-date facts, that they are decontextualized records of events, or that they use up all of the book-buying budget, wiping out the purchase of trade books.

Textbooks are hybrids in publishing, created for the particular purpose of helping teachers and students develop a curriculum for teaching and learning. They must be seen not as canons of culture, but as connected webs of ideas linking readers to common themes and issues. To be placed on an approved list, a textbook must be accepted by committee after committee, after being piloted and evaluated by districts and schools, and often reviewed in journals and periodicals. It is a miracle that texts make it through the vetting system at all, and no wonder liberal critics accuse them of being neutered and neutral.

However, textbooks can be useful to teachers new to given grades or subjects. They can act as road maps for the territory to be explored, even though they cannot be regarded as the curriculum itself. Some parents have watched their children work their way through every page of an assigned text, and seen a single book become a whole course. The pedagogy of textbooks is changing drastically in many classrooms, and the committees that approve or reject school books are cautious, aware of the difficulties in mandating books for students in a province, state, district, or school. Still, there are problems:

Author Pat Zettner was thrilled when one of the nation's leading textbook publishing companies asked to include her story, "A Perfect Day for Ice Cream," in its 1985 eighth-grade reader. Then she learned that a reference to Gloria Steinem had been purged because the editor felt it represented "militant feminism." The word "pest" was gone because it showed "sibling disrespect." "Kamikaze ball," referring to a soccer game, had been purged as a "possible ethnic offense."

Those changes paled, however, alongside others by another major publisher. That company changed the title from "A Perfect Day for Ice Cream" to "A Perfect Day," and eliminated a central trip to an ice cream parlor because it seemed to advocate junk food.

"It seems almost comical at first," Zettner said recently. "A textbook world in which no one must eat ice cream is an unreal world . . . . Its exclusion made my story — a single case among many — weaker and less vivid . . . . If ice cream can be censored, then what of apple pie? . . . My son Steven suggested that to preserve the thought behind the changes they should have retitled it, 'A Perfect Day for Broccoli Spears.' "

Elsa Walsh,
Taking Real Life Out of Textbooks

Until textbooks are changed, there is no possibility that crime, violence, venereal disease and abortion rates will decrease.

Mel and Norma Gabler,
Educational Research Analysts, Inc.

I hope I live to see the day when, as in the early days of our country, we won't have any public schools.

The churches will have taken them over again and Christians will be running them.

Rev. Jerry Falwell, President, Moral Majority

Modern public education is the most dangerous single force in a child's life: religiously, sexually, economically, patriotically, and philosophically.

Rev. Tim Lahaye,
The Battle for the Public Schools

A textbook is always the result of compromise. The question is, how much can texts be watered down in order to satisfy everyone? Some critics say that school books are so weak that they're on life support systems now, and if we continue to remove everything objected to by every group, from Christian fundamentalists to the politically correct gatekeepers, then children will have even less opportunity to read something significant.

We may well disagree with the opinions of would-be censors; unfortunately, they prevail in some areas. How can we cope with them, live with them, or fight them?

2. Issues in Censorship

It's impossible to shield youngsters from events around them. You can't send a child off to school, to the movies or to watch television and not expect him or her to be an ongoing member of the world with all its troubles and struggles. The notion of a child being immune to these matters while growing up in a well-protected home is a fantasy. Children are often stronger and tougher than we think. They're capable of more moral reflection and political savvy than we give them credit for. Children know about moral hypocrisy: They hear one line being preached and see another line being lived. So the matters we think we want to shield them from are part of their everyday lives.

I'll never forget the boy in Northern Ireland whose mother was Catholic and whose father was Protestant. All he saw were the struggles of a Protestant-and-Catholic world, one against the other. He kept saying to me how embarrassed Jesus would be if he were to come here and see what's going on in his name — this terrible fighting and hate. Though the fighting was tied up with religion, he saw how fraudulent it was. I thought, "Here is a shrewd moral and political observer at the age of 8 doing his work." This kid was no intellectual genius — just an ordinary kid who could take stock of what was happening.

Dr. Robert Coles,
"Horizons", *U.S. News and World Report*,
17 February 1986

Censors attack books for dozens of reasons, none of them easily classified. However, certain key issues and patterns recur in the different cases I have studied. We are used to the challenges from politically conservative or fundamentalist religious zealots. But in fact there are many religious leaders and conservatives who are firm opponents of censorship and who assist educators in fighting the attempts to ban books for children. And at the same time, liberal activists concerned about racism, sexism, and revisionist history are actively condemning books and texts throughout North America.

For a teacher or librarian, it is a shattering experience to find oneself the target of individuals and groups demanding the removal of books from the classroom or the school library. Of course, some cave into the pressure or assume they are guilty of misconduct. Others don't know how to respond. Still others want to fight back.

Family Values

Critics of literature are concerned that some books children read on their own or in school will weaken family resolve, faith, and strength in community. Defenders feel that books for children contain rich ideas that provide numerous opportunities for them to reflect on human nature. Thinking about the literature they read may help them to recognize the diversity of society and to build in their own minds ideas of what is acceptable and unacceptable behavior in their world. Characters in stories exemplify a broad range of behaviors and value systems, but they are representative of people we meet in life. When authors write stories in which characters may show negative features, they are not necessarily promoting such values. These stories and characters from literature represent the diversity of human experience and provide readers with opportunities to experience vicariously the total range of human qualities, alongside consequences of actions growing from various behaviors.

For example, in a short story, "Cheating", by Susan Shreve, a boy admits to cheating on a test, and is filled with remorse and guilt. His parents insist that he call his teacher and admit his misdeed. In the end, it is clear that the boy comprehends the consequences of his actions and accepts responsibility for them. And yet critics accuse stories such as this of demonstrating unfit behavior as a model for young people, encouraging them to lie and cheat.

In one case, a parent in Denver accused her children's schools and books they had read in them of turning her children against her. She cited the fact that her son was living with a woman of whom she disapproved, and that her daughter rarely visited her, as proof of the damage her children's education had done them. Whatever the reasons for her children's alienation from her, I doubt that what they read in school had much to do with it.

Stories for young people cannot always present perfect pictures of imaginary families. Good authors help readers reflect on why individuals must work at relationships in order to develop into socially healthy people. This is the role of literature, of real stories for real children, not contrived plots created only to paint a pretty moral.

I can't imagine anyone thinking that a teacher would ever permit the use of a story that condoned disrespect or undermined family values. One of the most common complaints of teachers is that children are disobedient and have no respect for authority.

Surely, we as professional educators, would not want to use any materials in our classrooms that would encourage the very behavior that we so often deplore. On the contrary, I have often used stories to illustrate how children should mind their parents, be respectful to their family members, and show kindness to others. Several of the stories tell of the consequences of disobeying family rules (a child develops a tummy-ache after eating too many of the cookies he was told not to eat).

Adrienne Elde,
Kindergarten teacher, Oak Harbor, Washington

Whole Language

In the 1970s, leading academics and educators began demonstrating that a "whole language" program might be the most effective method of teaching children to read and write. Under such an approach, children initially experience a story — not a text created by a textbook writer, but a real story not intended to "teach" anything — by reading it themselves or by having it read to them by their teacher. After this initial reading, students are directed through activities designed to prompt them to respond to the ideas, the sentences, the words, and other components of the story they have just experienced. A whole language program operates on the premise that children learn to read if they are interested in what they are reading. Thus, the stories used in a whole language reading program must be high-quality literary works that are likely to appeal to a child's interests and imagination. The activities accompanying each story are often discussion-centred, drama-based, and thought-provoking, designed to retain interest while teaching language arts skills.

A whole language reading program contrasts dramatically with a basal reading program (or series of primers), until recently the most commonly used reading program in the United States and Canada. A basal reading program aims to teach reading by first teaching the child the individual components of language (sounds, words, sentences, etc.) and then having the student put these components together into sentences. The reading selections used in a basal reading series are typically created by the editors of a textbook series in order to teach a particular reading lesson. As a consequence, the selections in a basal reading series often include overly simplistic stories that fail to interest children (witness the common criticism of the "Dick and Jane" readers).

This criticism of basal reading programs is now shared by the vast majority of professional educators. Books with a strong literary base, coupled with the whole language approach, provide authentic, meaningful language activities. Twenty years ago, educational authorities began revising guidelines to promote holistic language teaching, and wrote professional books giving teachers theory and pedagogy useful in promoting such a philosophy. Just as a child learns to talk through dialogue, he or she learns to read through interaction, listening to a story being read, commenting on the pictures and the print, learning what it is to become a reader.

In the whole language approach — which is, after all, the same approach taken by common-sense teachers for centuries — children first enter story by listening, learning how print sounds. Unburdened by the need to decipher symbols, they gain the immediate satisfaction of story from the beginning. Hearing exciting, powerful stories read aloud provokes their curiosity and arouses their desire to read print on their own. By building a classroom atmosphere that encompasses positive attitudes to reading, teachers can create situations where literacy is welcomed and cherished, and, most important, continued for life.

Stories grow in children's imaginations. Listeners begin to make connections between the outer world and their inner lives. Comparisons are made, motifs are understood. The story's relatives are recognized. Stories connect us, provide pathways for our journeys through life, crisscrossing our intentions, changing our directions, and illuminating our pasts and our futures. Story is a ritual that reinforces the interconnectedness of things, and the story repertoire that each of us builds forms a literary family circle.

When children are immersed in print they begin to think of themselves as readers. They quickly realize that print is rich in meaning and full of possibilities. By being inside the print, they begin to figure out how stories and poems work. The flow of language and the internal patterns and structures build print power. Dependably structured books guarantee children reading success. Books for beginning readers must propel them into anticipating what the words have to say, leading them to unlock print, with real language that complements their attempts to make meaning. Good books intrigue young readers, and draw them into the next line, the next page, the next book. They begin to have their own ideas about literary structures.

A wide selection of high-quality books from a variety of cultural settings will widen children's experiences. With the experience of reading familiar texts, their confidence and competence will continue to develop. Readers begin to understand the interaction of picture and text, to take risks with print by making informed guesses using a number of strategies, and language cues begin to mesh.

As I've indicated, the real intent of the popular emphasis on the mechanics of language — phonics, spelling, punctuation, grammatical analysis and rote drills — is to make sure that language is not used for those purposes of finding out and speaking out for which it principally exists.

To channel and illuminate feeling, to sharpen and enrich thought, a learner must have opportunities to plan and carry out projects, engage in open discussion, read widely, write many different sorts of discourse, solve problems, build things, and generally be free to apply mind and speech to internal and external matters. When children are permitted to do these things, it becomes impossible to control their thoughts.

James Moffett,
Journal of Educational Thought,
Vol.24, No. 3a, December 1990

The difficulty with the back-to-basics movement lies in the fact that the censors who advocate it want to limit students' educational experiences by focusing solely on simple skills — multiplication, grammar, memory work. They wish to eliminate time for classroom discussion on socially critical, realistic issues and ideas, and they see arts and literature as add-on frills. In 1989, Phyllis Schlafly stated that the major goal of her Eagle Forum was to "purge all journal writing activity from U.S. public school classrooms", surely a strange objective. Of course, language growth does not happen in isolation, but this is something many censors refuse to recognize, in spite of the evidence.

Diane Letsche taught Grade 1 in the early 1960s, long before whole-language learning came into effect. She then took 20 years off to raise her family and returned to teaching five years ago. Ms Letsche says she would never go back to the old system now that she has used the whole-language approach to teaching.

"I used to have a manual that said, 'These are the words you are going to introduce, this is the skill you will teach and when you get to Page ?? this is the question you are going to ask.' And you didn't dare let anybody turn the page to get ahead of you," says Ms. Letsche.

Now, she says, she reads stories and teaches words to her children that are relevant to them. For example, she says she often reads children the words in The Three Bears since the story is already familiar to them.

Ms. Letsche . . . sent one of her own daughters who had trouble reading to a tutor several years ago. The tutor specialized in phonetic education and her daughter's reading did improve. But Ms. Letsche says the improvement has more to do with the individual attention her daughter received than phonics drills. She adds that her daughter still has some trouble with comprehension.

"It's not whole language that is at fault," Ms. Letsche says. "It's the application of it that is at fault."

Ms. Letsche says critics of whole language should visit a classroom and see its successes.

There are 20 children that she taught last year that are reading and writing now. "There are 20 more that I taught the year before, and so on."

She adds that the relationship between students and teachers has changed. "In the old way, we thought of ourselves as the experts and the children as someone we were teaching. In the new system we see ourselves as co-learners. It's more humane."

Paul Waldie,
The Globe and Mail, 9 April 1991

This is a testament to the benefits of whole language teaching, but for every advocate there is an opponent. Newspapers and other periodicals have added much fuel to the fire with column after column attacking whole language and, often unknowingly, supporting the censors. But what are the goals of these attacks, and should we pay attention to them?

Schools were once part of a network of institutions that assumed joint responsibilities for bringing children to adulthood. Among these were the family, the church and the community.

The family, it seems now, is as likely to abuse and abandon its children as it is to love and nurture them.

The church suffers from institutional schizophrenia. Some of its members seem destined for irrelevancy, while others are indistinguishable from electronic con artists. And most of the population sleeps in on Sundays.

The community forgets that it's an organism and fractures into interest groups, competing jurisdictions and neighbourhoods more focused on their real estate value than their human values. But the schools . . .

When the lives of society's children cease to be a collective responsibility and when these same children, by virtue of their imperfections, intrude upon others, a scapegoat must be found.

Since all institutions but the schools have pulled a Pontius Pilate move regarding their obligations to children, the schools are left to take the blame.

The critics of public education have a litany of complaints. Among these are overpaid, under-worked teachers; a failure to teach the basics; and minimal standards. But the focus of their wrath is ill-mannered, ill-bred, illiterate students.

These students are our children; they are no more and no less than what we have collectively made them. They are less the products of the education system than they are the products of a society that absolves all but schools of responsibility for their flaws.

Today's schools shine brighter than their predecessors ever did. And there never was a golden age of education.

Michael Hume,
The Globe and Mail, 19 March 1992

If you agree with the sentiments expressed above, you will be upset by the following list of books challenged in public schools in Canada and the U.S. in recent years.*

Of Mice and Men by John Steinbeck
The Catcher in the Rye by J.D. Salinger
Who Is Frances Rain by Margaret Buffy
A Day No Pigs Would Die by Robert N. Peck
Brave New World by Aldous Huxley
The Wars by Timothy Findley
The Chocolate War by Robert Cormier
Forever by Judy Blume
Ordinary People by Judith Guest
The Diviners by Margaret Laurence
Slaughterhouse Five by Kurt Vonnegut, Jr.
Then Again, Maybe I Won't by Judy Blume
Impressions (reading series)

These books were banned, even though most of them are considered classics of literature. Do you agree that they should be forbidden for children? Or do you think kids should have the right to read these books for themselves? Your answer will reflect where you stand on censorship, child-rearing, education, and the very idea of what growing up is about.

Cultural Literacy

In their attempts at justifying the exclusion of certain stories for children in school, the evangelical censors turned to the writing of E.D. Hirsch in *Cultural Literacy*, a book in which the author created definitive lists of the literary selections an educated American should experience in school. Hirsch's list for every level from first grade through university was an attempt to define for educators cultural literacy, a knowledge of the place and time in which one lives, and an understanding of the implications beyond the stated context of what one reads. His work resulted in a wide-ranging controversy, from critics who disagreed with his exclusions, especially those representing multicultural minorities, to those who attacked the very notion of deciding what a nation must read.

---

* As part of its "Freedom to Read Week" program every year, the Book and Periodical Council publishes details on specific books challenged in schools and libraries.

Unfortunately, censors rallied around his concept of an approved list of reading materials, without understanding that he had included dozens of examples of the very books they were attempting to remove. Hirsch himself laments the development of reading materials that contain artificial or synthetic text, written by stables of authors hired by publishers to mass-produce paint-by-number stories. In fact, he has proposed that children be exposed to literature that is representative of our culture, stating that "although schools do comparatively well in teaching elementary decoding skills, they do less well in teaching the background knowledge that pupils must possess to succeed at mature reading tasks."

Hirsch, then, supports the case for a wide selection of literature, feeling that real literature can provide stories that allow children to explore and come to a better understanding of the world in which they live, and that cultural literacy is nurtured far more by reading good, solid, rich literature than by using reading materials featuring artificial text which is "skill-oriented". A story written around the sound "at", as in "fat . . . cat . . . pat", has little to offer most children.

The argument for cultural literacy works against censors, but lists of books deemed "worthwhile" seem a simple solution to the most complicated problems of educating young people in a cultural mosaic, and this is what they have latched onto in Hirsch's work.

The need for a variety of real books is shared by many, as witnessed by this testimony from Rabbi Richard J. Shapiro of Stockton, California:

> It is my clear impression that the purpose of the whole language approach is to foster reading skills using "real" literature instead of the artificial materials used when I was attending elementary school. As such, it is extremely valuable to include the wide variety of cultural traditions represented by the various stories in the anthologies. In this way our children not only learn to read but also become culturally literate, an attribute I find sadly deficient in our society today.

Witchcraft

One of the most contested issues involving stories in educational circles today is the charge of witchcraft or harmful interest in the occult. Surveys report a greater number of complaints about witchcraft than any other subject. Some minorities believe that devils and witches are a reality and a force for evil in the world, and they argue against any stories featuring witches. As well, a small group of self-declared witches who claim to practise pagan religions have begun to defend their right to free expression against critics — including authors of stories in which witches do not appear in a favorable light. Traditional Halloween tales have borne the brunt of the attack, and as a festive holiday Halloween has been banned in many educational communities.

It is inevitable: some literature does contain references and allusions to concepts that may be associated with a particular religious or anti-religious philosophy, bound to upset someone or other. But according to the U.S. Court of Appeals, inclusion in school courses of literature or artwork that contains such references does not constitute or even imply promotion of, or opposition to, any religion.

Some images or references in literature may inspire a hostile reaction from people with particular religious convictions. The sheer diversity of reactions reflects the plurality of family religious experiences and beliefs. Reading stories that include the religious beliefs of others does not constitute promotion of a religion, but encourages, according to the Court of Appeals, the "concept of freedom of religion, and intensifies the importance of developing an informed, enlightened, and tolerant electorate."

Scary Stories

Controversy about the inappropriateness of violence in books for young children has long been a subject for discussion. After protests by some psychologists, fairy tales were rewritten to temper the grim details that were once included. However, folk tales represent the plight of the human condition and are symbolic of good and evil. The horror may serve as catharsis for fears and anxieties that may be larger than those depicted in the stories. In Grimms' story of *The Seven Ravens* the little girl must cut off her finger in order to enter the crystal palace and save her brothers. Neither pain nor blood is described. In the broad context of the story the action represents the sacrifice of the girl who was partially responsible for the original curse placed upon her brothers. The rewards of the fairy tale are not easily won, and something must be given for each favor received. The monsters in *Where the Wild Things Are* by [Maurice] Sendak have been criticized for being too grotesque and frightening for young children. Yet children do not seem frightened of them at all. And the important theme of that story is that Max does return home where he finds the reality of warmth and love.

In some instances, books may be the very instruments by which children first encounter death or the horrors of war. How many countless children have wept over the death of Beth in *Little Women*, the necessary destruction of the faithful dog in *Old Yeller*, and even the end of a loyal spider in *Charlotte's Web*?

We should not deliberately shock or frighten a child until such time as he or she may have developed the maturity and inner strength to face the tragedies of life. However, literature is one way to experience life, if only vicariously. In the process a reader can be fortified and educated.

Charlotte Huck,
*Children's Literature in the
Elementary School*

Some of the most memorable stories for children are drawn from the world of shadows and suspense, of darkness and dampness, of the unknown and the unsuspected. The delicious feeling of fear, safe inside the surrounds of a story, can take us on adventures and journeys that make the hairs on the back of our necks tingle with delight. From a grandfather spinning a tale at the summer cabin on a hot evening, to a novel being read by a warm fire on a winter's night, story lets us wonder about things we would rather not meet in real life.

Beginning with peek-a-boo, moving into hide-and-seek games, and slipping into a sleeping bag at camp, children enjoy these stories full of creatures and events that populate our dreams and fantasies. We act out our adventures through playful stories, poems, songs, games, rhymes, riddles, and superstitions, recognizing the universal response to the switching off of the bedroom light, hoping for the glow from a night light. We relish these moments of mystery and suspense, which all human societies have always incorporated into their cultures — witness the shadowland of the Brothers Grimm, the fearsome Captain Hook, the nightmare of *Where the Wild Things Are*, the nightrides of Baba Yaga, memories of delicious chills and thrills. Childhood's fears can be framed inside the narratives of fantasy; children can recognize the ordinary and the fabulous components of a scary yarn. In the classroom, listening to a story read aloud, or reading a suspense novel on their own, they can join the circle of the community whose members know the truths of the stories, and share the thrill of being part of their telling. Perhaps scary stories belong in the end to children; they can be met and tasted and dissolved in an atmosphere of trust, before kids enter the world of adult life's problems. They take the pattern of the folktale, the campfire tale, the archetypal ghost story, and place them in storehouses for future meaning-making. Stories full of twists and turns, of mood shifts and night owls, of giants and heroes, help us to see patterns in our literature and in our lives as we weave the webs that will catch our future hopes and dreams.

Literature deals with many aspects of life which include violence, tragedy, and death — all of which may be viewed by some as demoralizing. Not acknowledging unpleasant things does not cause those things to disappear. Instead, stories featuring these topics can provide a vehicle for children to express their concerns and open new avenues for classroom discussion and writing.

In *The Child and the Book*, British psychologist Nicholas Tucker notes that occasionally a child may respond adversely to a story, but, while ". . .situations like this are bound to happen sometimes, [they] can best be modified by discussion afterwards rather than censorship before."

Lornei Chukovsky, in his study of Russian children "protected" from myths and fairy tales, says that these children created their own fantasy stories and worlds in place of the literature.

In *Choosing Books for Kids*, Joanne Oppenheim states that for eight- and nine-year-olds, "these are the years when tall tales with humorous exaggerations, fairy tales and myths are most appealing. Through such characters the child can encounter danger, overcome fear, taste courage, and triumph over all odds. The interest in fantasy and mystery for children ages 10-12 isn't so much seeking out the bizarre as it is a need to explore life and begin to face adult issues."

Bruno Bettelheim, noted child psychologist, reinforces the view that children can benefit and learn from stories and themes that may provoke some anxiety. Bettelheim states that "a particular story may indeed make some children anxious, but once they become better acquainted with fairy tales, the fearsome aspects seem to disappear, while the reassuring features become more dominant. The original displeasure of anxiety then turns into the great pleasure of anxiety successfully faced and mastered."

Children's emotional welfare and character are influenced by the significant individuals with whom they are involved. I believe their interest in scary stories is both natural and healthy. Dealing with childhood fears in fiction facilitates dealing with real fears when they are encountered. Even young children of these ages are readily able to distinguish between scary fiction and the real dangers they may encounter. Scariness is relative and situational, not an absolute attribute of a story, but the scariness of a tale depends on the perception of the reader. The essence of good literature is that it is open to a variety of interpretations. In Trina Schart Hyman's *Snow White* the dwarves are old and balding and arthritic. She changed my understanding of the tale forever with the personal statement she made through her illustrations.

> Let there be wicked kings and beheadings, battles and dungeons, giants and dragons, and let villains be soundly killed at the end of the book. Nothing will persuade me that this causes an ordinary child any kind of degree of fear beyond what it wants, and needs, to feel. For, of course, it wants to be a little frightened.
>
> C.S. Lewis,
> "On Three Ways of Writing for Children",
> *Horn Book*, 38 (October 1963)

Fantasy, Folktales, and Violence

The basic element in any fantasy is the creation of an imaginary alternate world ruled by its own laws and values. Although fantasy novels are set in magic realms, the laws and values they specify must be consistent and credible as well as recognizably human, so that the reader will understand and believe in the author's creation.

Fantasy worlds are inhabited by supernatural and mythical creatures such as unicorns, trolls, talking animals, and magicians. Authors may also create new beings or even new languages. Good fantasy writers are careful to describe the appearance and customs of their new worlds, which is why maps are common in the genre.

In most fantasy stories, the hero is a young boy or girl who must undertake a quest — a search that involves a journey — to find a powerful magical object, or to reach a special creature, person, or place to save his or her world from evil forces. The quest involves both physical and mental obstacles that challenge the hero's commitment.

Symbolism is an important element in fantasy. For example, rings and cups are often presented as powerful talismans of knowledge and truth. Common themes in fantasy include the triumph of love over hate, the conflict between good and evil, the search for knowledge or power, and the restoration of balance or harmony.

Like scary stories, these tales enable children to confront difficult issues in the safety of fiction, and yet they are often the object of attack by censors.

Imagination is an important dimension in the development of children's lives. Much of children's fantasy is positive, even delightful, and a necessary preparation for later life. However, there is also a dark side to children's fantasy and thinking, involving disturbing thoughts, fears, images, and nightmares. The harsh realities of modern life exacerbate these fears, but negative fantasies have been part of childhood experience for centuries. They are normal and almost always outgrown, but they are nonetheless real, and their power is reflected in the fearful elements in children's literature old and new, which helps children separate reality from fantasy as they develop control over their fears.

Critics have charged that some stories encourage violence or aggression in young readers. And yet when violence is depicted, it is generally not presented as an acceptable way of behaving, nor is it rewarded or condoned. Violence has been a common theme in children's literature for generations, allowing children to learn to control aggressive impulses, especially those involving family dynamics. Veronica is an outcast, a bully, who struggles to find her own way in *Veronica Ganz* by Marilyn Sachs. The children in *The Pinballs*, by Betsy Byars, arrive at a foster home after parental mistreatment, and they find a sense of family. The Inuit hero of *Dogsong* by Gary Paulsen attempts a rite of passage in the ice fields of the North. These stories all involve some kind of violence, and yet none of them could be said to condone or promote it.

Outstanding among today's children's authors, Richard

Kennedy has created stories with a fairy tale quality, peopled with fools, innocent maidens, wily old men, leprechauns, and clever children. His writing has been challenged in many different situations. In the story "Inside my Feet", a determined child battles to rescue his parents from an invisible giant. The tale has been attacked by many would-be censors.

A small passage of the story was printed in a letter to the Newport News-Times of May 22nd [1990], and the writer claimed it was excessively violent. The exact wording of the passage is this:

"the boots kicked and clomped, twisted, turned, and in a mad, frantic frustration banged me this way and that against the fence, until I was bruised and crying from the pain, holding on for life and in despair that there would be no end to the contest until my arms were torn from my body and I was carried off a horrible broken and bleeding stump to greet my mother and father without even the arms to hug them before we were brought to our end."

Well, it *is* violent, no question about that. But could this passage possibly fit into a larger story that would make it okay even if parts of the story *were* violent? A redeeming quality, you know? I hope so for the very sake of the bible itself, which is full of blood and gore and horror, but yet we excuse it because there is a loving god behind it all. For example, if all you knew about Abraham was that the voice of God told him to kill his son, and that he actually *attempted* to do it, you might say, "But that's *awful* stuff!" And of course you'd be right, it's quite insane and terrible. But if you know the whole story, and include the angel in it, and how the angel came down from heaven at the last minute, just as Abraham was about to thrust his knife into his son's heart, and then burn him up, and how the angel told Abraham that God was only kidding. . .. Well, then you might think that it was all okay, and that the "awful stuff" had a reason to be in there.

INSIDE MY FEET is a story with many good moral parts to it, and a few bad examples, like the PSALMS, and I fondly hope it has some good writing and decent characters, and surely it has an evil giant who lurks in darkness and who can send out for us, and will kill and devour everyone who cannot give the answer to his riddle, which is:

'WHAT BECAME OF THAT CHILD I WAS?"

The boy who is being so mistreated by the enchanted boots as quoted above is the hero of INSIDE MY FEET, and he must suffer some "awful stuff" in his mission to save his mother and father from a horrible death, and he must kill the evil giant, and you might excuse the violence in the story when you know all about that, and you might even guess the answer to the riddle.

But you must read the whole story for yourself, and not be satisfied to condemn it entirely when all you know about it is that little quotation. It is in the Impressions series, as noted. I hope you enjoy it, and your kids, too. And may we all be saved from evil giants. Amen.

Richard Kennedy,
letter to author

In *The Read-Aloud Handbook*, author Jim Trelease, one of America's most trusted experts on children's books, says this about Kennedy's story:

In an age of *Star Wars* and *King Kong*, it is a rare story that can chill middle-graders, especially a story about a giant. But this tale of a frightened but determined child's battle to rescue his parents from an invisible giant will have children on the edge of their seats. This giant is no pushover . . . he's mean spirited and awesome . . . yet he carries a heavy heart. To experience one of our great story tellers, pick up *Richard Kennedy: Collected Stories*, which includes this story as well as fifteen others.

Jane Yolen is perhaps best known for her tales of fantasy and fancy — what in *Touch Magic* she calls "those crafted visions and bits and pieces of dream-remembering [that] link our past and future. To do without tales and stories and books is to lose humanity's past, is to have no star map for our future." Many seemingly "scary" stories belong to the world of folklore. Folktales, "the stories of the tribe", provide powerful reading and listening materials for children aged eight to twelve. The context of "long ago" enables children to explore universal problems and concerns that have troubled humanity forever, but in a safe, nonthreatening framework. The deeds of heroes, the schemes of tricksters, and the lore of nations past can all serve as settings for children's own development through family situations, societal difficulties, supernatural beliefs, and natural phenomena. The learning and wisdom handed down through folktales can be understood and appreciated by today's children as they experience legends, myths, fairy and folktales retold and illustrated by contemporary authors and artists.

Stories of today are built on stories from the past. All modern writers write about themselves, just as the storytellers of old passed on stories that spoke to them and revealed images of themselves. A story can be read on many levels: a child reads it on one, an adult on another. The creators of modern literary tales for the young must recognize that children take their tales "to heart" — and so must their critics.

If you read fairy tales carefully, you will observe that one idea pervades them — peace and happiness can exist only on some condition or conditions, an idea which is at the core of our society's ethics, and at the core of international folktale.

Serious modern tales, borrowing characters and cadences from folktale, reflect both the individual and the society. Stories come out of and then go back into society, changing the shape of that society in turn, and modern myth-makers must not bear this burden lightly. Jane Yolen states in *Touch Magic* that "A story about a Prince would be historical. A story about a frog would be biological. But a story about a frog Prince is magical." The storyteller is an artist and selection is essential for art. There are thousands of characters, of details, of motifs. It takes great skill to choose from among them. Ancient humans took in the world mainly by listening — our world was shaped by oral traditions. The rememberers were the most attuned listeners — poets, storytellers, shamans, soothsayers. The carriers of the oral tradition were honored. Early childhood tales came from asking questions similar to those that children ask, and the best answers of the shamans, the storytellers, and the seers were collected in the oral tradition until they reached print. The storyteller or writer has always been part of his or her society, with the ideas and beliefs and prejudices of that particular society.

A tale well told forces a confrontation with the deepest kind of reality, giving children a focus, the very taste of primary truth. Story, then, is a primary act of mind. The best stories touch the past and the present in all of us, and yet none of them is exempt from banning: *Little Red Riding Hood*, for instance, is about danger, loss, and bravery; it has been banned in several counties in California, because in one award-winning version of the tale, the heroine carries wine in her basket.

There is a tendency today to try to protect children from all fantasy violence.

This is a mistaken notion, especially since more children are experiencing abuse or going through the pain of watching their parents divorce than ever before. We should not remove one of their important tools for coping with this kind of pain.

The child Matthew who has nightmares night after night is suffering, not because of the story he has read, but because of something in his own life. The story touches him in some way, giving him a way of dealing with some experience of question of his own.

Because they deal with universal fears and universal truths, fairy tales have been around for thousands of years. When small children ask for the same story to be read over and over, it is because that story is relevant to them in some way. Different fairy tales will appeal to the same child at different stages in his/her life. . ..

Reading about it in class can be a positive experience; in which the child finds out that he is not alone in his fear.

Even if we ban them from the classroom and the book stores, children will be telling each other fairy tales and horror stories as long as the human race survives.

Ann Ewa, The Toronto Star, 30 November 1992

Taboo Words

One of the most common objections to children's books is "inappropriate language", often labelled obscene or pornographic. Of course, students who use objectionable language have seldom learned to speak this way from books. Young people must be able to distinguish between literature and life, between the representation of reality in a book and reality itself. It is a common mistake to assume that if a character uses profanity in a book, the author advocates such words. In Lincoln, Nebraska, the school boards implemented a policy that states that "materials containing profanity shall not be disqualified automatically but shall be subjected to a test of merit and suitability." I agree with this policy, but many don't.

In French Lick, Indiana, in 1981, a high school principal confiscated copies of "Death of a Salesman" from eleventh grade students because, according to the principal, the book contained "vulgar language." The principal, who admitted that he had not read the play, said he decided to ban "Death of a Salesman" after several local ministers complained about it.

Edward B. Jenkinson,
Censors in the Classroom

My Friend Flicka, considered a classic since it was published in 1941, was pulled from grade five and six optional reading lists in Green Cove Springs, Florida because, according to some parents, it contains "vulgar language". The offending words were "bitch," referring to a female dog, and "damn".

Sexuality

As usual, complaints concerning sexual behavior in stories generally arise because the objectors feel that authors are not merely describing but advocating the behavior. Such descriptions seldom appear in literature for young children but are constantly surfacing in works for young adults by authors like Judy Blume and Robert Cormier. Controversial themes such as teenage pregnancy, premarital sex, masturbation, homosexuality, abortion, contraception, and AIDS do appear in some books for young adults, and teachers and administrators are often pressured to remove these books from schools. A highly vocal minority objects to artistic representation of any type of sexuality, and opposes the inclusion of any kind of sex education in school curricula.

Others argue that to deny students literature or even plain information about sex goes against basic educational principles. Because books for young people are often concerned with the emotional side of life, human sexuality can play a significant part in these stories. Writers and their publishers are extremely aware and concerned about the challenges to any mention of human sexuality, and most often deal with it with care and tact. Judy Blume's books have been read by millions of girls in the fifth and sixth grades, in spite of many teacher protestations. Kevin Major's *Dear Bruce Springsteen* raises the issue of boy-girl romance, and *The Man without a Face* by Isabelle Holland deals briefly with homosexuality. All have been attacked by would-be censors.

Secular Humanism

Censors from the far right define this term as being faith in humankind instead of faith in God, and claim that humanists have no moral values and, interestingly enough, no respect for free enterprise (!). Secular humanism is a catch-all phrase used to describe various ideas that don't jive with the views of creationists

— open discussion of ideas, clarification of values, sex education, discussion of evolution, and role play. In general, censors use this term to attack any teaching method that encourages students to think for themselves. By defining secular humanism as a religion, one supposedly opposed to fundamentalist Christianity, organized censors attempt to rid schools of discussion of any issues they find contrary to their own beliefs. One brochure put out by a fundamentalist group, Citizens for Excellence in Education, claims that public schools indoctrinate children with "humanistic" (i.e., godless) values through films, textbooks, library books, and courses on sex education, human sexuality, health, and family living. The brochure further claims that teenagers who indulge themselves in alcohol, drugs, sex, or satanism are encouraged by humanists in the schools and in the media.

Humanism [to quote from the brochure]:

- Denies the deity of God, the inspiration of the Bible, and the divinity of Jesus Christ.
- Denies the existence of the soul, life after death, salvation and heaven, damnation and hell.
- Denies the biblical account of creation.
- Believes that there are no absolutes, no right, no wrong — that moral values are self-determined and situational. Do your own thing, "as long as it does not harm anyone else."
- Believes in removal of distinctive roles of male and female.
- Believes in sexual freedom between consenting individuals, regardless of age, including premarital sex, homosexuality, lesbianism, and incest.
- Believes in the right to abortion, euthanasia (mercy killing), and suicide.
- Believes in equal distribution of America's wealth to reduce poverty and bring about equality.
- Believes in control of the environment, control of energy and its limitation.
- Believes in removal of American patriotism and the free enterprise system, disarmament, and the creation of a one-world socialistic government.

Humanism is referred to by Humanists as a "faith" and a "religion."

The Supreme Court has recognized humanism as a

religion. Does this religion have effective Sunday Schools? Not exactly. It has effective Monday through Friday schools. That's right! Our public schools. Our schools are rapidly changing from traditional education to "change agents" for Humanism.

Who pays for it? YOU DO!

This kind of rhetoric should be familiar to anyone who lived through the McCarthy era of the '50s. It allows for no differences, no agreement to disagree, among adults or children. In short, I believe it is fascist. It is also, at least for those who agree with it, very seductive because it promotes one and only one set of values — theirs.

Creationism

Many of those who don't believe in evolutionary science continue to seek to impose their religious beliefs on schools and want removed from the lists of government-approved science textbooks "those that include dogmatic teaching of a heathen philosophy supposedly supported by scientific evidence." In Texas the state board of education requires all textbooks that deal with the theory of evolution to identify it as only one of several explanations of the origins of mankind. Any material included in books on evolution must be clearly presented as theory, rather than fact. Again, the rhetoric allows for no disagreement: evidently church and state are not as separate as we thought.

In the next twelve months, California will establish state guidelines for the next generation of science textbooks for purchase by the state's school districts. Already the Creationists are threatening legal action if the requirements for the coverage of evolution are not watered down. In Texas, where the Creationism controversy flared again last spring, biology textbooks will be adopted at the state level next summer. Far Right organizations have promised to testify against any textbook that does not meet their sectarian standards.

People for the American Way,
Press release, 20 December 1990

Drama

Several types of teaching activities have been challenged by would-be censors. These include chanting in the early grades and role-playing (improvisation) at all levels.

In language arts classes, "chanting" refers to activities in which students are encouraged to read and compose stories and poems together. From little babies joining in "paddycake" rhymes with parents, to children in the playground participating in skipping rhymes, chanting allows children to be part of a whole, and encourages those who are less confident to join in language games. Through choral reading, chiming in, and call-and-response activities, children can bring words to life in a collaborative, cooperative activity. There is no hidden undercurrent of brainwashing or satanic ritual in oral reading and chanting in a classroom setting. How many of us remember with pleasure singing songs together in early grades? This is a form of chanting: should it be banned from contemporary schools? According to some, it should.

Children working in role are frightening to a small group of parents who feel that a child may not return to her or his real self once she or he has "tried on" the role of another person. However, drama offers children the opportunity to explore, to take risks, to be spontaneous and creative in a fictitious setting. To be educative, improvisational drama requires the physical, intellectual, and emotional involvement of children.

The situations that serve as starting points for improvisation may be suggested by children, initiated by teachers, or selected by either from stories they have read. The children must negotiate directly with other group members and their teachers, using language appropriate to the situation, and responding to and building on the ideas of the others involved in the drama. The teacher may work in role, or act as a side-coach outside the drama. The students may work in pairs, in small groups, or as a class.

In Canada, drama is considered a component of every language arts program, essential to a child's language development, requiring teachers to include dramatic activities drawn from provincial Ministry of Education guidelines on drama.

These drama-based activities are designed to encourage children to explore literary selections they have just experienced, to interact with their classmates, and to stimulate their imagination by encouraging them to create their own stories or poems. Research has shown that children learn more easily when they interact with each other, and yet many censors advocate that drama be eliminated from classrooms.

In Oakville, Ontario, a storyteller on a school visit was stopped in the middle of a performance by a group of parents and ordered from the school because her folktale included ghosts as characters.

In Kitchener-Waterloo, Ontario, the school board's drama policy was challenged by a parent group who claimed evidence of the role-playing of witches and other-worldly creatures. As a result an excellent document was drawn up by support staff describing the philosophy and the strategies for using drama in education with children, and explaining the learning that can result from role-playing fictional characters in an imaginary situation. Explanations like this provide parents with a rationale for school activities and help clear up some of their misconceptions about the study of arts in the classroom.

Political Correctness

Some stories are frequently attacked by the left because of their outmoded attitudes toward multiculturalism, the role of women, the physically challenged, racial, social, or sexual minorities, or religion. Politically correct censors wield increasing power; their views sometimes influence educators as much as those of right-wing fundamentalists. Can a woman be depicted as a housewife? Probably not. Can an anthology omit mention of people who are challenged in some way — blind, deaf, in a wheelchair? No. Can covers of texts show only children of white ancestry? Absolutely not.

Library materials considered to show women in demeaning roles were removed in the Salisbury school district in Pennsylvania. The Multi-Cultural Non-Sexist Advisory Committee of Cedar Rapids, Iowa, recommended permanent removal of more than 100 books, including such classics as *Mary Poppins, Dr. Doolittle,* and *Little House on the Prairie,* from the Kenwood Elementary School library, because they were thought to be racist, sexist, or biased against handicapped people.

In Ontario's Peel Board of Education, a poetry anthology I had collected was removed because of "The Lamb", a poem by William Blake that refers to the "Creator." (It should be noted, however, that literature representing cultures other than Christian are often included, such as creation myths, Egyptian tales, and Indian folklore, many descriptive of these faiths and their ceremonies.)

Political correctness is a hybrid issue, full of shadows and distortions alongside significant and powerful truths. The irony is that one of the primary goals of the politically correct — to accurately reflect the pluralist nature of our democratic society in the literature we give our children — results in stifling some of that very pluralism. *Huckleberry Finn*, for instance, contains racist views and characters. And yet I think it can be argued that it is a good book even though it reflects some of the harsh, bigoted views of the time its author lived in. Should we ban it forever, or should we help our children deal with an ugly historical reality through thoughtful discussion and analysis of it? More about this later.

Special Interest Groups

In Laytonville, California, the father of nine-year-old Sammy Bailey objected to his son reading Dr. Seuss's *The Lorax*, a story about preserving the natural environment (or, as *People* magazine called it, "the sad tale of a fuzzy little creature who loses his forest home when the greedy Once-lers cut down all the Truffala Trees"). Bailey senior, who owns a logging supply mail-order business in Laytonville, claimed the story demeaned the lumber industry. A full page ad in the local weekly urged the school board to remove the book from a second-grade required reading list. "Teachers . . . mock the timber industry," it read in part, "and some of our kids are being brainwashed. We've got to stop this crap right now."

In British Columbia, the International Woodworkers' Union attacked *Maxine's Tree* as representing a one-sided argument that countered the values and feelings of children whose parents worked in the logging industry in Canada. In the story, a family living in the Carmanah Valley goes for a walk in the woods and learns about clear-cutting. Signs are posted on trees to protect them, and Maxine puts her name on a tree and hugs it.

A teacher I know, working in a small mill town in Northern Ontario several years ago, began a study unit on pollution with his class. The next day, a letter from the local mill president arrived indicating his position would be terminated if he continued with the theme: he changed it.

3. Who Are the Censors?

Gene Maeroff, writing in the *New York Times*, calls them "The Book Cops." For the most part, censors are parents. Those of us who care about our children want to protect them as best we can, and with so many overwhelming horrors in modern life — drugs, teenage pregnancy, obscenity, pollution, AIDS, organized crime, war — how do we go about doing so? Do we follow legal proceedings, do we join radical causes, do we take matters into our own hands? Of course, we cannot protect our children either from the pain of real life or from ideas that we oppose. Katherine Paterson says that "to help your children grow strong enough for life is like teaching them how to walk through a forest strewn with land mines. But in the words of the old cliche no one ever promised us it would be easy." She then goes on to explain how mistrust of school and society in general can happen: "evil is very subtle, and parents are often duped." They may be drawn into signing a petition about banning school books because of claims of satanism, only to find out that the censors are discussing *The Lion, the Witch, and the Wardrobe*, one of the classic Narnia stories by C.S. Lewis.

Paterson's wise words tell us that we can only hope to help children develop through example, through "an awareness of the need for strength with which to withstand evil and to recognize good". When we help our children look at the world, difficult though that world may be, they will be equipped for their place in it. Paterson demonstrates compassion and tolerance for those parents who challenge ideas many contemporary schools represent, but she also states strongly that we must believe in a pluralist democracy, which, with all its imperfections, forces us all to allow others the same freedoms we ask for ourselves.

In a thoughtful article written for the Whole Language Umbrella Organization, Adrian Peetoom attempted to describe some censors, those parents who are so frightened for their children that they lash out and challenge the very books that may give their children awareness and protection. Peetoom feels that:

> some schools give parents the message that the past has been wrong and that the future's no longer guaranteed. Some of those parents see the trinity of the church, country, and school being broken for their children. They see schools proclaiming the need for students to be independent thinkers, but fear that what that means in practice is adults no longer loving God, country, and the primacy of American mankind.

Peetoom writes movingly of fundamentalist Christians and draws a picture — important for those of us who aren't — of those families afraid of losing what they believe they have struggled for. His compassion for them, as well as his analysis, have helped me make sense of important issues, and expanded my perception of why those who object to certain books in schools feel so strongly the need to ban them. Their worlds — whether they are left-wing radicals or right-wing fundamentalists — are under attack by the books their children are asked to read.

The People for the American Way, an organization that opposes censorship and advocates free speech, feel that the censors are engaged in a struggle for power, not morality. They believe that censors fear the spread of uncontrolled ideas and are threatened by the thought that the world is constantly changing, or that human beings have different viewpoints, cultures, and experiences. "They want sectarian control," as Adrian Peetoom writes. "There is a side to American Protestantism, especially within its fundamentalist, born again wing, which comes close to identifying American patriotism with Christian faith." Roger Rosenblatt, writing in the *New York Times*, says that America is and always has been a religious country even though it spreads its religiosity among many different faiths:

> Officially, America is an a-religious country: the separation of

church and state is so rooted in the democracy it has become a cliché. Yet that same separation has created and intensified a hidden national feeling about faith in God, a sort of secret undercurrent of religion which, perhaps because of its subterranean nature, is often more deeply felt and volatile than that of countries with official or state religions. Americans tend to treat every political dispute as a test of our national soul. The smallest incident, like the burning of the flag, can bring our hidden religion to the surface. The largest and most complex problem, like abortion, can confound it for decades.

C. David Lisman, reviewing the Christian private school movement in *Curriculum Inquiry*, says that Christian evangelicals are attempting to improve society through spiritual and moral redemption of individuals by isolating them from the mainstream: "The evangelicals want to impose their own view of moral redemption on society at large and this is especially where the danger for society lies."

In *Trust Your Children*, Leeann Katz writes:

. . . there is something in me that always feels a little protective of these people [censors]. I'm glad there are people who are obsessed with causes, and I admire their passion. Even though they may be the embodiment of intolerance, I think we need to defend their right to express their views but at the same time, we cannot allow them to take away our first amendment rights. It's a dynamic balance, and we have to work to keep it that way.

When channels are set in place for parents to opt in, when departments of education, school boards, and states and provinces spend time and money, recruit personnel, and struggle to find suitable books for children, then these parents will have to recognize the validity of the processes involved and find ways within the system to give their children what they feel they need, at school and at home. Most people appear to support public education that promotes a rich, diverse curriculum through which children of all ethnic groups and religious or non-religious persuasions can learn. Some, however, do not:

They are insisting, in fact, on a principle that public education seems founded on — the transmission of culture. In plain human terms fundamentalists are afraid of losing their children. They are saying, "Those books are not passing on our heritage and values. They are indoctrinating our children with someone else's way of life." Once again, they put liberals in a bind. Don't parents have the right to want for their children even what liberals disapprove of? Probably all parents, even the most liberal, fear this mental kidnapping by influences beyond the home. Here is one of the many contradictions in public education: we send our children to school to get for them something we can't give them at home, but we don't want school to change them from the way we made them. This creates the ambivalence that I find most characteristic of the public's attitude toward schooling in general and literacy in particular. As parents we claim we want schools to broaden our children's minds and teach them to think for themselves, but we don't completely mean that. We all have our assumptions and limits. The fundamentalists are franker; they know they don't mean it.

James Moffett,
Journal of Educational Thought,
Vol. 24, No. 3A, December 1990

Who are the censors who want to control the stories which I as a teacher want to share with children? Of course there's no easy answer to that question.

The Far Right Censorship Network

The number of national organizations in the U.S. encouraging censorship and attacking public education grows every year. They boast strong local affiliates, financial backing, newsletters, "how-to" manuals, and powerful leaders. In the research, I notice that individual organizations are constantly changing their names, but among the groups with the most influence are Jerry Falwell's Moral Majority, Phyllis Schlafly's Eagle Forum, The Pro Family Forum, The Heritage Foundation, and Mel and Norma Gabler. The Gablers operate Educational Research Analysts Inc. in Longview, Texas. They provide research for local activists across North America in leading censorship crusades. Certainly, in the field of textbooks, the Gablers are the most influential censors America has ever known. As well, their reviews of stories have sparked controversies in every state of America, and in Canada, Australia, New Zealand, and Japan. Their philosophical stance includes reinstating traditional sex roles, rewriting history, denying scientific theory and replacing it with Biblical creationism, and banning all discussion of subjects such as segregation, human sexuality, women's rights, trade unions, the civil rights movement, slavery in America, world hunger and poverty. They are especially against open-ended questions asked by a teacher after telling students a story because they might promote secular humanism. They feel that books that encourage students to come to their own conclusions are not fair to children or parents: "A concept will never do anyone as much good as a fact."

Originally the Gablers organized to influence the Texas textbook adoption process. However, their impact soon spread throughout North America, and books were being criticized by people who often had not read them or even seen them. One health text was found objectionable because it included a brief mention of national health insurance. Another social studies text was removed because it considered the importance of federalism rather than the idea of strengthening the power of each state.

Always in the Gablers' reviews are these two concerns: 1) until textbooks are changed there is no possibility that the rate of crime, violence, venereal disease, and abortion will do anything but continue to climb; 2) textbooks mold nations, because textbooks largely determine how a nation votes, what it becomes, and where it goes.

Here are some examples of specific criticisms levelled by the Gablers against books, as reported in *Censors in the Classroom* by Edward B. Jenkinson:

From a teacher's guide: "You might then discuss what they feel is the responsibility of our society toward minority groups (e.g., requiring by law that all curbs be slanted so that people in wheelchairs can have access, etc.)."
Gabler objection: invasion of privacy. The text is attempting to delve into the personal values of students.

"Segregation because of race has been ruled illegal by the United States Supreme Court. What other kinds of segregation can you think of? Should all kinds of segregation be prevented?"
Gabler objection: invasion of privacy. This question deals with student values and is inappropriate for the classroom.

"Who earns the income in a family? Who is the 'head' of a family? Who has the most to say about rearing the children? There is no one answer to these questions today. More than one family member might be

employed. It may be hard to decide exactly who is the 'head' of a family."
Gabler objection: this is an attack on traditional family roles. To
satisfy the women's movement, this creates lack of respect for men
as heads of families and is an assault on the religious beliefs of many
people.

A discussion of gun control in a school text.
Gabler objection: The text is obviously in favor of gun control
which is evident from the quoting of a member of the National
Rifle Association as favoring. In the eyes of the student this would
nullify much of the influence of the NRA, which has fought so hard
to protect citizen rights.

*"No one knows exactly how people began raising plants for food instead
of searching out wild plants. . . . Perhaps a person in some long-ago
(hunting/gathering) group had a favorite kind of food and began to give
those plants special care where they were found."*
Gabler objection: the text states theory as fact, leaving no room
for other theories, such as the Biblical account of Cain as a farmer.

"Millions of years were needed to form these fuels from decayed matter."
Gabler objection: many people do not believe the earth is millions
of years old.

*"Find out how school rules are made in your school. Find out how they
can be changed. Describe the procedure to your classmates."*
Gabler objection: the text stresses change. This teaches children
dissatisfaction with rules and encourages a desire to rebel. Why
assume that students will want or need to change rules?

Robert Simonds is a former pastor, high school teacher, and
principal. In 1983 he founded the National Association of Christian Educators. Its mandate insisted that the children of America
receive the very best education possible in both academics and
moral and spiritual values. Through his Citizens for Excellence
in Education (CEE), he advises people who object to certain textbooks in school districts throughout the United States and, on
occasion, in Canada.

Simonds believes that he is involved in a war between secular
humanism and Christianity, nothing less than a struggle for the
heart and the mind and the very soul of every man, woman, and
— especially — child in America. He believes that for Christians,
neutrality does not exist. His scheme is to elect Christians to

public office. Booklets from his organization include "How To Start a Parent Group", "How to Deal with School Boards", and "Tips on Writing Good Press Releases". He believes that a winning strategy is only as good as the abilities of the believers to carry it out. He is adamant about including Christianity in children's books, while his opponents see such messages as religious propagandizing. CEE see themselves discriminated against in school texts.

In *Educational Leadership*, Simonds laments that America is pluralistic:

> . . . we wish it were all Christian, but living together in tolerance of others' views — such as humanism — does not mean we will be neutral. Satan's use of the word neutral is phenomenal. The ACLU calls for "neutrality" in public schools — translation: No Christian religion or belief is allowed — only the neutral philosophy of "irreligious" secular humanism. Those who would follow neutrality in any life situation are spiritually immature. For Christians neutrality does not exist.

Simonds' influence extends to Canada. In 1990, a group of parents in Manning, Alberta successfully lobbied their school board to have the reading series *Impressions* removed from local schools. Shortly afterward, Hana Gartner interviewed Simonds on the CBC program "the fifth estate".

Hana Gartner: Do you take some credit for what happened in Canada?

Bob Simonds: We have a fairly large mailing list in Canada of people who need help and we give them the research that we've done. . . I really do think that some of the people who wrote those stories are sick minded people. I really believe that because . . .

Hana Gartner: Rudyard Kipling, A.A. Milne, Dr. Seuss?

Bob Simonds: Hey, sure. They have . . . they're no dummies. These people are not dumb. They're just . . .

Hana Gartner: Evil?

Bob Simonds: I think their minds are warped by the very simple fact that they reject God.

Throughout the '80s, parents organized dozens of book burnings throughout the U.S. Among those burned: *Snow White*, *The Living Bible*, *The Hobbit*, and *The Sun Also Rises*. The February 1983 issue of *The Pro-Family Forum Newsletter* contained the following advice: "It just may be that Hitler's burning of anti-Nazi books prior to World War II has made us have an unholy respect for anything printed in book form. Just because a book has been published does not mean that it has an eternal right to exist or to be read . . . some things must be kept, and yes, some things may be burned."

Liberals and Censorship

At the other end of the political spectrum, liberals find themselves in a quandary when it comes to censorship, bringing to the battle deep and unanswered questions about their own impulses to censor books for young people. Many censors on the left either are sympathetic to or come from embattled cultural or racial minorities which feel they are already threatened — sometimes physically, sometimes socially — by other forces in society. They may not be as organized as the right, but their concerns are as deeply felt; they believe that their values — pluralism, tolerance, multiculturalism — are under attack, and like the fundamentalists, they sometimes think that an author who uses ugly language or deals (in the "wrong" way) with issues such as racism or sexism is proselytizing rather than describing.

> Extremist racist speech is an assault on the psyche of those it targets. It threatens the physical security of victimized communities, and aims to destroy societies that are open and pluralistic. The law must remain as an instrument available to a multi-cultural democracy to protect itself against the hatemonger.
>
> Manuel Prutschi, Executive Director,
> Canadian Jewish Congress,
> *The Globe and Mail*, 3 September 1992

School texts are being scrutinized by forces on both the right and the left. History books, in particular, have been attacked by revisionists, and defended by those who frame the work within a particular cultural context. For example, in the textbook *Canada: A Story of Challenge* by J.M.S. Careless, we read that "The labors of the Jesuit fathers that ended in martyrdom were a tremendous effort to win savage, half-comprehending people to Christianity and civilization." This sentiment is no longer acceptable to educators attempting to lead young people to an understanding of the European arrival in North America. Attempts to change a traditional, sometimes biased view of history, as marked by the controversy over the 500th anniversary of Christopher Columbus, have had an impact on all cultures, not always leading to a clearer view of events. In Mexico, an official school history text has been rewritten to present a view of Mexico that fits with the views held by the ruling party. However, the book is less critical of the United States, and critics attribute the change to the government's desire for a North American free-trade agreement. As well, the text includes a glowing portrayal of the administration of the current President of Mexico.

Some parents are upset by the continuation of school Christmas concerts. Traditional songs and ceremonies are being replaced with faith-neutral celebrations of cultural heritage. Since no religion is supposed to dominate in the multicultural climate of today's schools, many parents are disappointed, some with loss of Christian religious representation, but others because they valued the literature, the songs, and the history inherent in the celebration of Christmas. Who is right? Is there a way to include specific religious literature in classes without threatening the self-respect of children who are not members of that particular religion?

Huckleberry Finn represents the complexities involved in selecting and censoring books for young people. While it is regarded as a masterpiece by many, some parents are offended by the book's use of pejorative labels for blacks; still others offer Mark Twain's satire as an attack on the racist attitudes of his time. Many school boards in Canada and the United States have removed the book from courses of study, especially those for junior high school students, citing the need for an understanding on the reader's part of the author's intentions. Some school boards have developed print resources for teachers to help them cope with the inherent difficulties of teaching the book. (Similarly, guidelines were created by officials at the Stratford Theatre Festival in Ontario to assist teachers in discussing the performance of *The Merchant of Venice*, deemed anti-semitic by many Jews.) One author worries that removing books to protect our children may in the end make young people more vulnerable:

> This point was made by Dr. Kenneth Clark, a distinguished psychologist, during one of the times that *Huckleberry Finn* was under attack by a group of black parents. Kenneth, who is black, argued that when you prevent black kids from reading this book because it contains the word "nigger," you are telling them that words are so powerful that you can't do anything about them except hide them or run away from them. He said that's not the way to deal with racism. The way to deal with it is to learn about it and explore its motivations, not run away from it.
>
> Nat Hentoff,
Trust Your Children

The suggestion that the novel *Lord of the Flies* is racist and should be removed from Toronto schools has surprised the book's London publisher and some people in Metro's black community.

> The offending passage comes from Piggy before the others tear off his glasses and kill him.
> "Which is better," Piggy asks. "To be a pack of painted niggers like you are, or to be sensible like Ralph is?"
>
> *The Toronto Star*, 25 July 1984

Lord of the Flies had been a popular book for classroom study until a group of parents told a Toronto Board of Education committee that the book is racist and should be removed from Toronto schools. The parents said that they didn't want racist epithets taught "in the area of English Literature".

Perhaps a more eloquent critique came from Miguel San Vicente, a parent who said there were "racist undertones throughout the book. There's a bias against people who hunt, a whole tone of bias in favor of Western civilization, against people of tribal cultures, for want of a better term." Such comments raise issues of deep concern to many liberal parents today, but I believe they should lead to discussion, not banning.

Another current phenomenon in books for children is the desire to satisfy the hunger for ethnic variety. As multiculturalism sweeps the world of children's literature, there is demand for books featuring multicultural characters and issues. But who will write these stories? The question is really, "Whose voice may an author use?'' Can a WASP write as if he or she were a Catholic? Can a white European write in the role of an Amerindian? Can a man portray the feelings of a woman?

Concern about negative stereotypes leads naturally to the question of "cultural appropriation". Should a non-Chinese interpret Chinese folktale, should Europeans or their descendants try to retell native legends? Canadian author Claire Mackay stated that she was at a total loss for words when one member of an audience asked her how any non-native could realistically hope to write about a North American native at this time in history. She feels such sentiments are "pure censorship masquerading as political correctness." Does the charge of cultural appropriation deny writers the right to explore cultures different from their own?

In the Kamloops, B.C. school district librarians recently began removing the novel *The Indian in the Cupboard* until its contents could be reviewed. It was challenged as being potentially offensive because, though written by Englishwoman Lynne Reid Banks, it tells a story of a plastic Amerindian figurine that comes to life and befriends a nine-year-old boy. It won the 1984 Young Readers' Choice Award of the Pacific Northwest Library Association and the 1985 California Young Readers Medal, and the sequel to it was given the Parents Choice Award and was named one of the notable books of the year by the *New York Times Book Review*.

The school district sought legal advice on whether it had the authority to place a sticker on copies of the novel stating that its contents might offend some readers, but Lynne Reid Banks threatened to sue if such a label was placed in any of her books, and the educators relented. The controversy will continue, and some liberals find themselves in the position of acting as censors of books for children.

At a recent Writers' Union of Canada annual meeting, Timothy Findley defended writers' freedom of expression against "all types of censorship, be they from the right or left." But a compromise was worked out so that the union membership voted to reject the idea of appropriation, choosing instead to condemn "cultural misappropriation".

We will have to come to grips with this problem of voice with our consciences and our souls, for the argument is not simple. For too long so many voices were silent or not allowed to speak. Perhaps in the future each group will find representation, and we will be able to speak our thoughts in the safety of fiction from the point of view of any role we need to use for our purpose. Certainly the Canada Council's idea that it is preferable to study and even consult a community foreign to one's own when creating fiction about it is a sensible one.

The agony of censorship, of choosing what is right for all children — not just our own — will continue. What is perhaps heartening is the fact that the debate about the subject is becoming increasingly public. As long as it isn't hidden, conducted behind closed doors by faceless proselytizers or educational bureaucrats, there is hope for some resolution. Everyone involved may have to compromise, but the ultimate result will be a victory for all of us.

4. A Case Study of Censorship

The Impressions Story

Along with four other author-editors, I began to create *Impressions* in 1978. Today, it is used in both public and parochial schools throughout Canada and the United States. One out of every two Canadian elementary schoolchildren has used books in the series.

My fellow author-editors and I began to create *Impressions* by first gathering high-quality works of children's literature to include in a reading series. During our search for appropriate literature, we focused on selecting works by critically renowned, award-winning children's authors and illustrators. Putting together anthologies and teacher resources for the classroom was a project full of difficulties: we had to balance the needs of different communities and groups within them, avoid stereotypes, feature characters of both sexes and various racial and social backgrounds — in short satisfy common educational standards that have become the norm all across North America. I can't describe all the twisting and turning we did, the agonizing over individual selections. Suffice it to say that not one of us was motivated by a desire to propagate a particular political or religious point of view; our main aim was to find superb stories that would inspire children to read. Period.

We read thousands of poems and stories, from books, magazines, and other texts; we searched through school libraries, public libraries, book stores, and reference materials, and we actively sought the advice of experts who had made children's literature their life's work. We used a variety of procedures in selecting the stories, poems, and illustrations. For example, we examined each selection to determine whether its level of difficulty was suitable for a particular grade level, whether it reflected the cultural diversity of North American society, how it portrayed men and women and special needs children, and, of course, whether it could be used effectively to teach language arts. A committee of teachers and consultants then read these choices and tested them with children for interest and readability in order to narrow the material down to a manageable amount. In short, developing the reading series for Kindergarten through grade six took dozens of devoted people years of work. The result is a collection that includes the artistry of more than 500 writers, poets, and illustrators who allowed us to use 800 selections in order to bring internationally acclaimed literature, classical and contemporary into the classrooms of North America.

Impressions was quite a stretch at the time of its publication in 1984. It was more than just another reading or language art series. For a publisher to risk using real books, written by authentic authors, to put up all the monies for permission fees, to be multicultural, with stories from England, Australia, America, and Canada, was a brave undertaking.

We didn't create *Impressions* for the U.S. We made sure that our content was 40 percent Canadian and the best we could find at the time. Gradually, the books began to leak across the border as American teachers visited or attended conferences. Soon the publisher was getting requests from the west coast and from states bordering on Canada for other copies. Eventually, of course, the company decided to print and distribute the books in the U.S. More and more, school districts are determining which texts they will use drawn from an approved list, while in the past, an entire province or state would "adopt" a text, and every schoolchild read those books. Amazingly enough, districts in California adopted our books. This was when the trouble started.

The Challenge to Impressions

It is difficult enough to get a school textbook accepted throughout Canada; getting it into the American market only to meet the California version of political correctness was quite an achievement.

However, teachers, principals, and state authorities wanted the books in America. By 1988 the series had been adopted by about 100 districts in California for use in their Kindergarten through grade six classes. Since then only four have conceded to the challenges detailed below and stopped using the books.

Early Challenges

The controversy over *Impressions* first erupted during the 1987-88 school year in small communities in Washington (Gig Harbor) and Oregon (Troutdale), and other towns in the northwest. The critics complained that the books had overtones of witchcraft, mysticism, and fantasy, and represented persistent themes of child rebellion against parents and authority figures. Other challenges stated the series was depressing and violent, and still others objected to Canadian spellings and references. One parent stated that the books could serve no purpose except to introduce "our children to witchcraft step by step".

Impressions had been chosen in the districts concerned after a thorough evaluation over several years, with much time for community involvement. Teachers felt that *Impressions* was the only series that met the standards they had decided were important. But the demands to remove the books persisted, and in Troutdale the books never made it into the schools. In Oak Harbor and Gig Harbor, in the state of Washington, after costly battles, the books were retained. A cluster of national far right groups directed the attacks against the books — the American Family Association, the Christian Educators' Association, Citizens for Excellence in Education, and the Traditional Values Coalition. Robert Simonds, head of CEE, had declared war on the series and urged chapters of his organization to demand their removal wherever they were in use. The main objective was to bring public education back under the control of the Christian community — or at least one part of it. The publication *Citizen*, from the organization Focus on the Family, included an article on the series entitled "Nightmarish Textbooks Await Your Kids". The form of the objections varied, but they often included lifting passages out of context, or distorting the content of the entire series by representing only one theme — for example, Halloween. As well, objections focused on the teacher resource books and the student activity books, which accompanied the series and were optional for teachers. Among the challenges were various sinister interpretations of imaginative stories, along with fears of occult and Satanic hidden propaganda, such as numbers and faces that could appear when books were held upside down, against windows, or in mirrors. As well, *Impressions* bore the brunt of the anti-whole language movement. It must be noted that there were many parents, teachers, and students who supported *Impressions*. For school districts that had made their decisions carefully, setting their goals and evaluating materials that would meet those goals, and working alongside parents, the challenges represented costly and emotionally exhausting months of debate. Because of the network of the far right, other districts and communities began to receive the pamphlets and newsletters, and hear the attacks on *Impressions* from the Christian networks on radio and on television. Challenges were brought against books in eighteen districts in California alone, as well as in Washington, Idaho, Alaska, Ohio, Illinois, Nevada, South Dakota, and New York. The books were rejected for adoption in Georgia, North Carolina, Oklahoma, and Mississippi.

The first major incident occurred in Portland, Oregon, where I was grilled one morning by a group of parents accusing me of including stories promoting witchcraft in the series. However, in the afternoon I met with a group of witches who were very upset that the stories did not portray them in an accurate light. Such is the conundrum of censorship. Which witch is which?

Over the last few years, I have encountered angry parents and hostile media; I have even adopted a disguise to walk through a threatening crowd carrying signs that read "Booth Leaves a Bad Impression". In this "holy war" some people working on their own have fought in immoral and illegal ways. They have threatened boycotts of local businesses that supported school systems using *Impressions*. They have brought audio or video recorders to board meetings without prior approval and edited the tapes for their own purposes. They have initiated recall from office of elected representatives, school board members, and superintendents. They have sent free curriculum materials to teachers attempting to bypass districts' materials selection procedures. They have demanded immediate removal of materials to avoid adherence to district policy and procedures. They have sent anonymous hate mail. They have started destructive rumors about people with whom they disagree. They have brought into communities far right "experts" on Satanism and witchcraft who used guide books and training manuals designed to help people recognize devil worshippers. They have claimed that those who disagree with them are unpatriotic, anti-Christian, anti-family, pro-Satan, or pro-communist. They have flooded local newspapers with carefully timed and orchestrated stories and letters. They have asked for educational personnel records in order to attack particular teachers and administrators. They have violated election laws by placing campaign signs in illegal places. They have entered classrooms with tape recorders without clearance from school offices. They have torn posters, signs, and flyers from school bulletin boards. They have threatened school personnel with bodily harm. They have left intimidating messages on pro-school activists' telephone answering machines. They have constantly claimed they represent the values of the whole community.

The Charges of Witchcraft

Although I had heard of historical accounts of witchcraft such as the Salem witch trials during the seventeenth century, I did not know of, much less was I familiar with, any modern-day religion of wicca, witchcraft, or neo-paganism when I helped to create *Impressions*.

I also know each of the other author-editors personally. I have spent numerous hours over several years in meetings with each of them when we were creating *Impressions*. None of my fellow author-editors ever mentioned witchcraft, wicca, or neo-paganism to me at any time.

At no time did I or my fellow author-editors ever select any work appearing in *Impressions* because of its connection with any religion, sect, or cult. From my extensive experience within the textbook publishing industry — including having had several of my own works published and sold for use in public schools throughout Canada and the United States — and my knowledge as a professor of education, I knew when I was creating *Impressions* that including any religious material would cause public school authorities to reject the series. In fact, in creating a series for use in Canadian public schools, I was required to comply with very strict publishers' guidelines set out by the Ministry of Education in each province to prohibit the inclusion of religious, racist, or sexist material in public school textbooks. I therefore excluded religious material and other controversial matters from the series. My fellow author-editors were likewise aware of these guidelines and were especially careful to not include any religious material.

But the far right thinks the series advocates witchcraft. Many of the stories, illustrations, and accompanying activities to which plaintiffs have objected reflect the "Mystery and Adventure" theme present in each of the six grade levels represented in *Impressions*. These selections are intended for use in the fall, and thus depict witches and other images often associated with common non-religious cultural observances around Halloween. Witches also are common characters in children's literature and folklore, and are often deliberately used in children's stories to symbolize mysterious and sometimes evil things. Typical of this genre are such classical stories as "Hansel and Gretel", "Snow White", and *The Wizard of Oz*. One of the selections in our series, "The Wicked Witch of the West", is a work of prose based upon a character in *The Wizard of Oz*. That witches appear as characters in some of the selections in *Impressions* is due to their prevalence in children's literature and folklore. In each instance where we included a selection in which a witch appears, we did so to serve a non-religious, educational purpose.

For example, "Dear Country Witch", "Witch Goes Shopping", and "Bedtime Stories" are a series of selections by the same author, Lilian Moore, that relate to the "Mystery" theme. We included a number of poems by one author to help children develop an awareness of the poet . "Dear Country Witch" is a variation of a famous children's story, "City Mouse and Country Mouse" and thus teaches children that a variety of stories are possible on the same theme.

"Witch Goes Shopping" is intended to contrast the folkloric witch with the concerns of modern reality. It helps to point out to children the difference between fact and fantasy in a humorous fashion.

WITCH GOES SHOPPING

Witch rides off
Upon her broom
Finds a space
To park it.
Takes a shiny shopping cart
Into the supermarket.

Smacks her lips and reads
The list of things she needs:

"Six bats' wings
Worms in brine
Ears of toads
Eight or nine.
Slugs and bugs
Snake skins dried
Buzzard innards
Pickled, fried."

Witch takes herself
From shelf to shelf
Cackling all the while.
Up and down and up and down and
In and out each aisle.
Out come cans and cartons
Tumbling to the floor.
"This," says Witch, now all a-twitch,
"Is a crazy store.
I can't find a single thing
I am looking for!"

Again, we did not include selections with witches to promote, endorse, or signify approval of, or, for that matter denigrate witchcraft or any religion. Yet in the court trial in Woodland, California, "Witch Goes Shopping" appeared as evidence for the plaintiffs.

Lilian Moore is one of the most widely respected children's poets in the world. In the encyclopedic *Children's Literature Review*, she is honored with seven full pages describing her accomplishments. The author of dozens of poem anthologies and picture books, Moore is the recipient of the NCTE Award for Excellence in Poetry for Children. Critics praise Moore for her economy of language, evocative imagery, and natural, unforced style. Both poems by her included in *Impressions* are referred to in critical reviews as representing the best of her writing.

"Witch Goes Shopping" presents a list poem for children to pattern. Chanting is an acceptable activity according to every single language arts text on the market today. Both the poet and the *Impressions* authors understand the symbolic and archetypal use of the term "witch", and reject any attempts to connect this whimsical, imaginative piece with Satanism.

The authorities in the wicca religion supporting the parents gave depositions that stated that the witch's broomstick represented a circle of phalluses that she rode around in an orgy of Satanic lust. However, on reading the poem, the reader may agree that their viewpoint rests in hysteria. And yet:

> Thomas C. Jensen, Police Officer in San Jose: ". . . researched and investigated the occult since 1985 . . . interviewed over two hundred teenagers involved in or dabbling in the occult . . . spoken on local and national television and lectured around the San Francisco Bay Area on "Teenagers and The Occult."
> . . . the *Impression* series is a breeding ground for the occult, involving ritual activity such as chants, spells, lighting candles in a circle and fortune telling. This activity is all consistent with witchcraft or the Wicca religion."
>
> Deposition for trial, Woodland, California

Adaptations

Challengers expressed concern that the *Impressions* series uses adaptations or retellings of "traditional" stories, apparently centring on the misconception that there is "one right version" of traditional literature.

Folk and fairy tales come from the oral tradition and were not collected in written form until late in their history. Like all traditional literature, they were preserved from generation to generation by the common people through storytelling. Their origin, as Lillian Smith notes, "is lost in the mists of time".

Through repeated tellings and retellings, the stories became lean and polished. They survived because of their vitality and their ability to "give expression to deep, universal emotions — joy, grief, fear, jealousy, wonder, triumph." At several grade levels, the *Impressions* series considers material adapted for various media. From time to time, we ask children to adapt material for a radio broadcast or to prepare a television story board.

One challenge concerned a scene from *Anne of Green Gables*. The passage in the text was taken from the libretto of the musical by Don Harron, based on the novel *Anne of Green Gables* by L.M. Montgomery. The teacher's manual points out that several movie and television versions have been made based on the story.

The version is included to illustrate the way material can be adapted for various media.

Impressions includes the song from the musical version of Anne to present children with an opportunity to make the words come to life, and to see how one story can make several stories.

Impressions did not change any lines. The rights were purchased from Don Harron because the authors felt strongly about including *Anne*, but in a new mode. The musical had run successfully in Prince Edward Island for many years.

Without making it clear that we had used a respected adaptation of the book, the complaints started.

Even the CBC got into the act. On "Radio Noon", an interviewer, Christopher Thomas, discussed the series with an irate parent.

Parent: They were talking in the original story about the earth, she [Anne] wanted to know why it was red. In the original story they were describing about why they thought it was red, and so on, but they've changed it. Now Anne says, "Do you suppose that it could be the wounds of tragic destiny dripping from a blood-stained family tree? An evil spell that did compel the founders of the Island to meet with their doom and perish horribly. Picture now, the vicious strife that started way back in the olden days of yore. Family fighting with family, feuds engaging, drenching all the local soil with gore." And that's not in the original.
CT: Not the *Anne of Green Gables* I remember, no. But, in terms of your children, what has been the impact from the kind of thing?

The next day, the host clarified the source of the adaptation. (He might also have pointed out that the quotation is perfectly typical of something Anne might have said, in the novel as well as the play.)

Aboriginal Writings

There have been challenges concerning anti-Christian writings relating to Native American myths and culture. For example, "Day and Night" is based on an Inuit myth regarding creation. "Initiation poems" are Zuni Indian parables about coming of age in Zuni society. "Zini and the Witches" is a story by a contemporary author based upon a Native American myth. Teachers read such stories in their classrooms because of their literary value and because they expose children to other, minority cultures in our society. In Canada, every public school reading series is required to include selections from both Inuit and Amerindian cultures. We did not include these selections in order to promote or advance any religious views. But there were inevitably charges of neo-paganism.

Mapping the Challenges

It is important to chart how most groups worked to fight the series. Each case was slightly different — the reason for the complaint, the modus operandi, recourse to legal action, etc. — but there were also some striking similarities. They are instructive, and should interest anyone who wants to fight on either side of the censorship debate.

Willard, Ohio

In Willard, Ohio a group of fundamentalist Christian parents, represented by the American Family Association Law Center, filed a lawsuit against the school board and school superintendent seeking over $1 million in damages and requesting that the federal district court declare that the school district's use of these books violated the Constitution. The plaintiffs claimed the books promoted witchcraft and the occult, and that by using the books, the school district had established the religion of witchcraft placing a religion in the school curriculum, an unconstitutional act in the United States. A motion was filed for a temporary restraining order, asking the court to excuse students from reading *Impressions* and to provide alternative reading materials. The court denied the motion and indicated it would not grant other injunctive relief in the case. The People for the American Way joined the school district's council in providing legal representation for the school board and the school superintendent.

Charges in the Willard, Ohio case included the following:

- One plaintiff charged that the series promotes the "New Age" religion because it contains pictures of and references to rainbows, described as a "New Age symbol". "I feel this program is step-by-step teaching our children to look to the rainbow. There is a mind control program being used in some schools using the colors to

evoke certain emotions and feelings. I don't approve of this . . ."
- A woman objected to an illustration of more than thirty people dancing and playing, because it included two groups of three people — two women and a child, and two men and a child. The plaintiff argued that the illustration "depicts homosexuality".
- Other plaintiffs objected to a story in which a boy describes his dog as a good friend. One argued that the story depicts "inordinate affection for animals". Another objected to it because "we are created human beings and have been given dominion over animals . . . we are more than animals."

Yucaipa, California

Nowhere has the *Impressions* controversy raged more violently than in Yucaipa, California. The debate involved parents' groups, teachers' associations, schools, right-wing religious organizations, the National Teachers' Union, and the school district offices, which were constantly picketed in 1989-90. School board meetings were packed in an effort to persuade trustees to remove the books from the classrooms. Disturbing flyers were sent around town claiming that stories in the series had been adapted to include references to violence and mutilation. Trustees listened to hours of testimony at four consecutive meetings. Forest L. Turpin, executive director of the Pasadena Association for Christian Educators' Association International, said his organization was for Christian teachers who work in public schools, and its purpose was to ensure that Judeo-Christian ideas would not be lost. "Many parents sent their evaluations of the series to us and we help them to understand how to unemotionally and effectively articulate their own concerns. The Bible says we're the ambassadors for Christ. The question is how to do that in a pluralistic society." Good question.

The religious activists charged the schools with promoting everything from Satanism to homosexuality. They picketed the schools, harassed teachers, and attempted to recall two of the school system's five school board members. The voters returned the board members to office after nearly a year of acrimony, but the damage was done.

Both sides in the protest fought to the end. School board supporters took their message to the streets; more than 600 teachers and parents lined Yucaipa Boulevard.

After hundreds of hours of testimony and scalding public debate, the school board voted to retain the series. Alternative core literature classes for those students whose parents did not wish them to be involved with *Impressions* were set up at elementary schools. Parents enrolling their children at school sites completed written forms making their individual choices for their children's language arts program. *The Wall Street Journal* reported that, "In Yucaipa, teachers who have used the books have been threatened and have seen their homes and cars vandalized, and some teachers who use the texts were physically threatened. Others found nails pounded into the wheels of their cars."

South Dakota

Controversy raged in the Sioux Falls and Douglas school districts 1988-89. Two school board members said they had received letters warning them that opponents of the series would work against their re-election if they didn't vote to have the books removed from schools. They said they would vote against bond issues and find suitable school members to replace those who refused to comply. The school board received petitions with 1,700 names asking that the books be removed, and 20 parents filed formal complaints against the district. When the Douglas school board decided to keep the series, there were telephoned death threats and vows to "cut the heart out of the superintendent John Sweet and his principals." Secretaries in the school office heard on the phone chants of blood and gore along with a number of obscenities. The *Rapid City Journal* reported that one teacher was grabbed by a Douglas parents' association member and told, "the prince of darkness will get you." But the books remained in the schools.

Dixon, California

Debbie Fraser, the wife of Reverend Richard Fraser of Dixon Community Church, led the opposition to the books on the basis of religion. She presented the board with a petition signed by 278 residents within the school district who wanted the series removed. A crowd of about 450 concerned parents and residents heard opposing views about the series at the school district meeting. One parent complained her daughter had the first nightmare she'd ever had after reading some of the stories. Another parent stated that children learn their values at home. "My kids don't sleep with the light on and the door open because of what they learn at school. They sleep with the door open because they were taught that way." The board voted to retain the series; the decision was met by a standing ovation and cheers.

Woodland, California

Unlike the preceding challenges, this one went to court. The ruling by Judge William Schubb of the U.S. District Court in Woodland, California, near the state capital, Sacramento, created a legal precedent throughout America. The controversy centred on whether the texts violated the separation of church and state guaranteed in the first amendment of the U.S. constitution. The American Family Association Law Center filed the suit on behalf of a Woodland couple, Douglas and Katherine Brown, alleging that the series promotes, sponsors, and endorses witchcraft as a religion, later amended to allege that it also promotes neo-paganism, and that this constitutes an attempt to establish a state religion, a violation of U.S. federal and California law. The plaintiffs were parents of schoolchildren enroled in the Woodland joint unified school district in grades three and six.

The defendants declined the court's invitation to participate in one final settlement conference in order to resolve the dispute, apparently preferring the costs and uncertainties of litigation and appeal to the process of mutual accommodation.

Before adopting *Impressions*, the school district had evaluated the series and three others in a lengthy piloting and review process during the 1988-89 school year. The process included field testing of the different textbook series by teachers at all elementary school grade levels, meetings between principals and teachers using the new series, and teachers who were not involved in the piloting process. As a result, nine of the twelve elementary schools selected *Impressions* as part of their language arts curriculum.

In the end, the judge ruled in favor of the school district. This court case may act as a precedent, inhibiting small groups from challenging textbook adoptions that are the result of legitimate public and school processes.

Canada

In British Columbia, when the series was challenged by a group of concerned parents in 1991, the Ministry of Education created a study group of parents, educators, and administrators from across the province to examine the materials and bring forward recommendations. After deliberation the Ministry accepted the group's work and *Impressions* remained in the schools of British Columbia. In supporting the decision, the Canadian Library Association reiterated its belief in both the freedom to read and the freedom of parents to have access to what their children are reading.

In most communities in Canada, the debate was begun by one or two parents in a school district and then was passed on by local board administrators. Hamilton, Ontario is an example where a school board trustee decided to publicly attack the program in a local newspaper and the ensuing series of letters fuelled the controversy. In most cases, the debate was resolved and the series retained in the schools. Sometimes, however, arguments became violent.

Manning, Alberta

The most serious attack of censorship, perhaps in Canada's history, involved a small town in northern Alberta, where parents of twenty-eight families "stormed their children's school, held the principal captive in his office, and then cleared the classrooms of allegedly satanic materials. The offending literature it turned out, was a decade old series of school readers called *Impressions*, which contained handsomely illustrated selected stories, poems and even scripts" (*The Globe and Mail*, 26 February 1992). It was a truly violent debate growing out of the American network that had fuelled the controversy over the last five years. Two Roman Catholic parents from the town had attended a Sunday school convention and come back with the information on *Impressions*, the reading program that had been used in their children's school, Rosary Catholic School, for the previous two years. Eventually, in spring 1991, a group of parents became concerned and approached the school to ask that *Impressions* be removed. The board commented that the staff had agreed to use the series. The parents pursued the complaint at the provincial level, resulting in the agreement that an alternative series would be put in place within a year. However, on the first day of school in September 1991,

> thirty parents appeared at the school demanding that the books be withdrawn immediately. They walked into the school and demanded that the books be removed from their children's sight or else they would burn them forthwith. One said I don't care if I go to jail. I want those books out of there. Wendell Darringer, the principal of Rosary School, attempted to contact his superintendent, Lachlan Phimister, but parents tied up the phone, called Phimister themselves and again demanded that the books be removed from the school. The superintendent told the principal to remove the books pending further discussion by the board. Within a couple of days, the school board held a meeting by telephone conference call and agreed to remove the series from the school permanently. When the department of education asked superintendent Phimister why he hadn't called the police and charged parents with trespass, he said it was better for his school and community not to push things to that degree. But in the meantime parents had used inquisitional tactics in confronting teachers prior to September, and the argument had spilled over into the school yard, in fights between children of opposing parent groups.

> Peter Carver,
> Freedom of Expression Committee of the Book and Periodical Council

As we have seen, the national media picked up the story, and parents and educators throughout Canada realized the enormous implications of censors taking procedures into their own hands. For me, this event was a watershed: support for *Impressions* in Canada grew as media commentators, editorial writers, journalists, and school authorities demonstrated concern and offered directions for the future. Canadians had begun to see the danger of book banning in schools.

What these stories all show is the recurring patterns in attacks on books, who is often behind them, and who will help opponents of censorship. But how will we combat censorship in the future?

5. Fighting Future Battles against Censorship in the Classroom

Lessons and Successes

What does the future hold for those of us who work with children and books? At a time when communities have become conscious of the need for literacy among children if they are to become lifelong readers, we find the very stuff of literacy at the centre of bitter controversy. Faced with would-be censors on both the right and the left, schools must select books with extra caution and care. And as libraries find themselves under budget constraints, who will preview the books? Who will help us select appropriate titles for the children in our care? If texts come under attack from censors of all kinds, what will the children read?

The communities that have been successful in defending books under attack have organized support networks to help develop a rationale for the use of those books. The secret of the future of print in North America lies in the partnerships among parents, teachers, authors, publishers, libraries, and, of course, all readers.

The stories children remember live beside the stories of their families, alongside the stories of their friends, and next to the stories authored by others. We cannot value one over the other. Each and all are part of the storying world that we inhabit from birth to death. It takes so many stories to become human — some spill out, some are forgotten, others remain only as bits and pieces. But in the sifting and sorting of our story lives we will always be developing our story sense, and as we retell one from memory, the remnants of others will haunt the present one and color it with hues unimagined. In the galleries of our minds, the stories will touch each other, rub against each other, alter shape and substance, mix metaphor and symbol, become the ordinary and the fabulous all at once.

We must celebrate the children who teach us anew every time we share a story with them. We must celebrate the teachers who plunge into story pools with children. We must celebrate the authors and illustrators who write down, retell, invent, and illuminate stories from and for all of us. But most of all we must sing the praise of the story — that most simple and complex creation of all the arts.

I no longer argue with the censoring groups. Our positions are opposed. But I still enjoy talking to parents who have questions and worries and concerns about their children and about the literacy experiences their children should have in school. I realize that labels aren't very useful, that Christians come in all sizes and colors, that all atheists or Jews or Buddhists don't necessarily share the same concerns for their own children. When I worked recently with one hundred children in a school in my area, I saw every skin color possible, heard dozens of languages and bits and pieces of cultures very unlike my own, and yet very similar. It thrills me always to see story draw us together in such a tight circle, the eyes of the children wide open, and their minds making sense of what the story holds for them, reflected by everything that has ever happened to them. The community of storying people is precious to me.

I still read stories about ghosts. I still read tales of witches. I still love roaring like an ogre, or whispering words in the dark. They are part of the heritage of all of us who have left the caves, worked the fields, and huddled together at dusk. We make meaning from what we hear and read because of what our lives have given us, and we take those stories and construct our very lives with them. And each one of us creates a personal story, backed up by our own home and value system. That's the magic of storying. That's the safety net for working with stories and other people's children. It must be very frightening to be afraid of story, to fear the world so much.

I am more frightened by the anger on both sides of the issue, by the intolerance both groups feel toward each other. I also understand the frustration of a teacher, following ministry guidelines and board documents, and using material recommended for the children in her care, when she is challenged by censoring groups. And I can grasp the concern of parents who want the stories and poems their children read and listen to represent what their community deems best for the cultural literacy of its children.

There are stories I no longer read or have children read in school — the Bible (not permitted by school codes), stories containing blatant sexism or racism, stories without much meaning for today's children. But should children choose to read those selections, they must have access to them somewhere, in the home or in the library. I have never been afraid of print. My parents believed in reading and I was allowed to read what I wanted. I seemed to know what interested me the most, what I could handle, and what was suitable. So does my son.

I have compassion for parents concerned about their children's education and well being. How could I not? We set in place department of education guidelines, board of education committees, consultants and advisors, parent committees, all responsible for vetting the resources available to the schools, and we must make those committees as wide-ranging and as comprehensive as possible. They will represent the culture of our schools. The books we read will reflect that culture, and while the school community may seem a disparate one, it is nonetheless a community of children, parents, and teachers, engaged in a common activity — the education of children.

To achieve that goal, I believe it is vital to allow individual children to choose what they read, if necessary with their parents' approval. But what worries me is the loss of what we call our shared experiences, the songs we sing together, the stories we listen to together, the poems we say together. For many children, teachers are the books in their lives. We bring to them the print that matters. We are the stories they read. School culture, for too many children, represents the only print power in their young lives.

For many children the censorship battle makes no difference. They read no books, they hear no stories, they sing no songs. Columnists in the newspapers clamor for a return to the basics, when millions of children get *only* basics in school. And to learn to read without meaning, to never know that print has power, to never sense authorship as a reader or writer, to not be part of the group silence that greets a moving story — it is these children whom school loses.

Organizing against censorship takes many different forms in communities across the country. Tactics and strategies vary depending on the level of community concern and involvement, available resources, the interest level of local media, tactics used by the opposition, the particular materials in question, and the school systems' level of preparedness.

A sampling of the successful anti-censorship efforts suggests the variety of approaches that can be used:

- In Corvalis, Oregon, a new citizens' group, People for Public Education, was formed.
- In Girard, Pennsylvania and Calhoun, Alabama, the authors of books under challenge were brought in to address the local communities.
- In Sylvania, Ohio and Widefield, Colorado, public education campaigns were led by school administrators.
- In Baileyville, Maine and Island Trees, New York, lawsuits demanding banned books be returned to classrooms were filed by students and parents.
- In Tell City, Indiana, teachers, board members, administrators, and parents united to respond to false charges levelled at the schools by the censors.
- In Louisville, Kentucky and Fort Lauderdale, Florida, People for the American Way's anti-censorship film was shown on local cable television and at community meetings.
- In Texas, Minnesota, and Wisconsin, state-wide anti-censorship coalitions were formed.
- In Elkader, Iowa, a librarian enlisted national and local support from educational organizations to help maintain access to books and ideas.
- In Beverly, Ohio, a teacher started a class in which parents read and studied controversial books their children would be reading.

Preparing for Battles over Censorship

Looking ahead, it seems to me that many local communities have become better equipped in recent years to combat attempts at censorship and other attacks on public schools. Increasingly, school districts are developing review policies and procedures to address local challenges.

Schools are gradually changing the manner in which they

handle challenges to books being used in their classrooms. Educators are realizing that school, home, and community are not enemies in educating children, but members of an interdependent partnership. Given the pluralist society we live in, there can never be complete agreement about what constitutes effective education. But this complication must not obscure our basic agreement on the fundamentals necessary for helping children to be secure in their learning environment. We who work in schools must gain the trust and confidence of the parents of the children we teach, so that they can support their schools and their teachers, enabling us to create a strong basis for curriculum and curriculum materials, and help us when individual parents are confused or angry about our programs. Those school systems with community support, through parental involvement, will be better prepared to deal with controversy when it arises.

Today educators are less likely to panic when faced with a complaint by a parent or an outsider about a book or a text used in their schools. In the past, to avoid publicity or confrontation, a book was often removed from a school because of one challenge. Today, school districts and individual schools are taking a much more organized and constructive approach. And the emphasis should be on organization: most successful attempts at censorship have been organized efforts; so should the efforts to stop them. The list of suggested actions that follows has been drawn from several sources, including my talks with teachers and parents over the last five years. The points of information may be useful in developing a policy at a school or district level for coordinating battles against censorship.

1. When parents voice a complaint to a teacher or principal, they must be listened to carefully, in hopes that the problem can be clarified through discussion, stressing the partnership of home and school in the community, in order to reduce tension. It may be necessary to move to the next step, receiving a complaint in written form, or speaking before a school board meeting. But the local school board should be the course of last resort. By having a policy in place, school officials will have the time and background to make informed, rational decisions. The various steps in the procedure, as well as the appeal process, should be described carefully and explicitly for both teachers and parents.

2. Parental concerns must not be mocked, minimized, or ignored. Schools have to consider the needs of the whole community in their philosophical approach to learning resources.

3. A school board must never give up its legal rights in an attempt to mollify an angry group. As much attention as possible should be focused on directing complainants to central district offices, away from children and teachers. This promotes consistency in school responses, and protects the children from involvement in confrontation.

4. Authorities handling the situation should resist debating in the media the opponents of a particular book or series. When the media become involved, the community's needs are often lost in the blare of publicity.

5. Everything officials say will be made public by their opponents, in one form or another; this may be true even of statements made in private or in confidence. Be prepared to have those statements taken out of context or misinterpreted, or even used with the opponents' message to make a point directly opposed to your own.

6. When dealing with complainants, remain as polite, patient, and soft-spoken as possible. Emotionally laden language is often the medium of the challengers, and reasoned, thoughtful policy is the hallmark of successful rebuttals.

7. Books and materials under attack must be considered innocent until proven guilty.

8. Officials will have to be prepared for challenges of deliberate deception, and charges of far-ranging conspiracies. Any admission of mistakes on the part of officials will be seen as part of a plot to keep parents from having a say in the lives of their children.

9. Parent advisory groups can be very effective in dealing with censorship issues. Members must understand their advisory role and accept the group's level of power and limitations. It is important to listen to other groups who may be supportive as well. Book review committees should have broad representation, including members of the community, parents, teachers, and administrators. As well, the focus of the

advisory group should be on assessing the educational merit of the challenged material.

10. The criteria for selecting books and other instructional learning materials should be shared with parents at an early stage in the selection process, so that parents who wish to be involved can have their questions answered before the books are selected.

11. Children should not be involved in any dispute. Such action can only inflame the opposition, and bring charges of poisoning children's minds.

12. If the complaint is of a religious nature in a secular school setting, then the positions on both sides may prevent negotiation or compromise. Since opponents may not change their positions, it is vital that the policy in place for handling censorship challenges be followed carefully.

13. Each challenge must be carefully examined in order for the issue to be clarified for both parties. Often blanket statements are used to promote an entirely different accusation. A half-truth, an exaggeration, or false information must be exposed, so that parents will hear the facts presented as truthfully as possible.

14. Use resources and networks to gain information about past censorship challenges to the material, the organizations behind the challenges, legal rulings on similar charges, reviews and commendations for the materials. Contact support groups for moral, legal, and financial backing in the struggle.

15. Challengers, in an attempt to be taken seriously, will often claim support from the entire community. It may be necessary to involve other individuals and groups to combat the claims of the censors. Such sources of help include:
    • home and school associations;
    • civil liberty organizations;
    • feminist groups;
    • unions;
    • church groups;
    • writers;
    • broadcasters and journalists.

16. As teachers, we must be mindful of rumors and gossip spread in censorship battles, and remain professional with children and parents on all sides.

17. As school programs alter, more and more books will be found inside classrooms. If texts have to be vetted by dozens of committees, then who will assist us in knowing the thousands of trade books that students may eventually have access to in school? It is far too dangerous and simplistic for each teacher to try and find "safe" materials. Instead, we will have to be informed members of teams of educators, working with each other to build awareness of and responsibility for what children read and talk about in school. It is disheartening to hear some teachers say, during a censorship controversy, "Let's just drop the book and use something else." When schools and teachers are empowered to determine their own resources, when the community feels it has a significant role to play in its schools, then challenges will lessen as responsibility and collaboration grow. For those few who want their children to have an education situated inside a particular religious framework, there will have to be alternative or private schools.

As I stated at the beginning of this book, it is intended to be only one small contribution to our ongoing debate about books and children. If nothing else, I hope it leads to discussion and argument, as well as community involvement.

For years, schools attempted to keep matters of censorship quiet. But censors know well the power of publicity, and parents and teachers must learn to illuminate the actions of those who are working in the darkness, attempting to control book selection without free discussion. We need to become involved in our children's lives, in their freedom to read and to know. We need to struggle to keep books in our schools, to know those books, and to trust in our selection.

We want to become literate so that we can choose what we want to read and write about. Our own stories will live beside the stories of our families and our friends, in the shadows of the stories authored by those we have never met, but whom we somehow recognize, as friend or foe. Each and all are part of our story world. In making and remaking them, we are all the time developing our story sense and constructing our world. The stories that stay with us are those that connect us to as wide a world as possible, and yet illuminate our own heritage and our private family. We are, of course, our stories all together.

LIBRARY

Organizations to Contact

The following brief list describes a number of organizations fighting for the freedom to read:

In Canada:

Book and Periodical Council
Freedom of Expression Committee
35 Spadina Road
Toronto, Ontario
M5R 2S9

Canadian Library Association
Advisory Committee on Intellectual Freedom
Metro Toronto Reference Library
789 Yonge Street
Toronto, Ontario
M4W 2G8

In the United States:

American Booksellers Association
560 White Plains Road
Tarrytown, NY
10591

American Civil Liberties Union
132 West 43rd Street
New York, NY
10036

American Library Association
50 East Huron Street
Chicago, IL
60611

Freedom to Read Committee
220 East 23rd Street
New York, NY
10010

International Reading Association
800 Barksdale Road
Newark, DE
19711

National Coalition against Censorship
2 West 64th Street, Room 402
New York, NY
10023

People for the American Way
2000 M Street N.W., Suite 400
Washington, D.C.
20036

References

Ajzenstat, Sam, and Michaelle McLean. "Censorship: Two Views". *Artviews*, Winter 1984-85.

American Booksellers Foundation for Free Expression. *Censorship and First Amendment Rights: A Primer*. Tarrytown, NY: American Booksellers Foundation for Free Expression, 1992.

American Library Association. *Intellectual Freedom Manual*. Third edition. Chicago: Office for Intellectual Freedom, American Library Association, 1989.

Anderson, R.C., E.H. Hubert, J.A. Scott, and I. Wilkinson (eds.). *Becoming a Nation of Readers: The Report of the Commission on Reading*. Washington, DC: The National Institute on Education, 1985.

Berger, Melvin. *Censorship*. New York: Franklin Watts, 1986.

Bettelheim, Bruno. *The Uses of Enchantment: The Meaning and Importance of Fairy Tales*. New York: Vintage/Random House, 1977.

Birdsall, Peter, and Delores Broten. *Mind War: Censorship in English Canada*. Victoria, BC: Canlit, 1978.

Books on Trial: A Survey of Recent Cases. New York: National Coalition against Censorship, 1985.

Booth, Jack, et al. *Impressions*. K to Grade 7. Toronto: Holt-Harcourt Brace Jovanovich, 1984-1988.

Boyle, Kevin (ed.). *Article 19 World Report 1988: Information, Freedom and Censorship.* New York: Times Books, 1988.

Briggs, Katharine. *The Vanishing People: Fairylore and Legends.* New York: Pantheon Books, 1978.

British Columbia Library Association (BCLA). *Intellectual Freedom Handbook.* Burnaby, BC: BCLA Intellectual Freedom Committee, 1989.

Bryant, Mark (ed.). *Publish and Be Damned: Cartoons for International P.E.N.* London: Heinmann Kingswood, 1988.

Burstyn, Varda (ed.). *Women against Censorship.* Vancouver: Douglas and McIntyre, 1985.

Bushe, Charles H. *An Intellectual Freedom Primer.* Littleton, Colorado: Libraries Unlimited, 1977.

Canadian Children's Literature. An Issue on Censorship: No. 68. Guelph: Department of English, University of Guelph, December 1992.

Carver, Peter. *A Cautionary Tale.* Toronto: Book and Periodical Council, 1992.

Collins, Janet. "Suffer the Little Children," in *Books in Canada*, October 1991.

Comber, James P.M.D. "Should Censorship be Allowed?" in *Parents Magazine*, July 1990.

Davis, James E. (ed.). *Dealing with Censorship.* Urbana, Ill.: National Council of Teachers of English, 1979.

de Grazia, Edward. *Girls Lean Back Everywhere: The Law of Obscenity and the Assault on Genius.* New York: Random House, 1992.

Dean, Malcolm. *CENSORED! Only in Canada.* Toronto: Phenomena Publications, 1981.

Del Fattore, Joan. *What Johnny Shouldn't Read.* New Haven: Yale University Press, 1992.

Dick, Judith. *Not in Our Schools?!!! School Book Censorship in Canada: A Discussion Guide.* Ottawa: Canadian Library Association, 1982.

Douglas, William O. *Freedom of the Mind*. New York: Doubleday, 1964.

Egoff, Sheila, and Judith Saltman. *The New Republic of Childhood*. Toronto: Oxford University Press, 1990.

Gillespie, John T., and Corinne J. Naden. *Best Books for Children: Preschool through Grade 6*. New York: R.R. Bowker, 1990.

Goldberg, Dr. Susan. *Times of War and Peace: Dealing with Kids' Concerns*. Toronto: Annick Press, 1991.

Goodman, Kenneth. *What's Whole in Whole Language?* Portsmouth, NH: Heinemann, 1986.

Haight, Ann Lyon. *Banned Books*, fourth edition. New York: R.R. Bowker, 1978.

Harrison, Barbara, and Gregory Maguire. *Innocence and Experience*. New York: Lothrop, Lee and Shepard, 1987.

Hearne, Betsy. *Choosing Books for Children: A Commonsense Guide*. New York: Delacorte, 1981.

Hendrickson, Robert. *The Literary Life and Other Curiosities*. New York: Viking, 1981.

Hentoff, Nat. *The Day They Came to Arrest the Book*. New York: Laurel-Leaf Dell, 1982.

Huck, Charlotte S. *Children's Literature in the Elementary School*, third edition updated. New York: Holt, Rinehart and Winston, 1979.

Index on Censorship. London: Writers & Scholars International Ltd. Issued six times a year.

Jenkinson, David. "Censorship Iceberg — Manitoba," in *Canadian Library Journal*, Vol. 43, No. 1, February 1986.

Jenkinson, David, and Pat Bolger. "The Role of the Reviewing Journal", in *Canadian Materials*, vol. XVIII/3, May 1990.

Jenkinson, Edward B. *Censors in the Classroom: The Mindbenders*. New York: Avon Books, 1979.

Jenkinson, Edward B. *The Schoolbook Protest Movement: 40 Questions and Answers*. Bloomington, Ind.: Phi Delta Kappa Educational Foundation, 1986.

Landsberg, Michele. *Michele Landsberg's Guide to Children's Books.* Markham, Ontario: Penguin, 1985.

Lipson, Eden Ross. *The New York Times Parents' Guide to the Best Books for Children.* New York: Times Books, 1988.

Lurie, Alison. *Don't Tell the Grown-ups: Subversive Children's Literature.* Toronto: Little, Brown, 1990.

Lynn, Ruth Nadelman. *Fantasy for Children: An Annotated Checklist and Reference Guide,* second edition. New York: R.R. Bowker, 1983.

Marsh, David. *50 Ways to Fight Censorship.* New York: Thunder's Mouth Press, 1991.

McCormick, John, and Mairi MacInnes (eds.). *Versions of Censorship.* New York: Doubleday, 1962.

Meade, Jeff. "A War of Words," in *Teacher Magazine,* November-December 1990.

Meek, Margaret, et al. *The Cool Web.* London: The Bodley Head, 1977.

Mertl, Steve. *Keegstra: The Trial, the Issues, the Consequences.* Saskatoon: Western Producer Prairie Books, 1985.

Mitgang, Herbert. *Dangerous Dossiers: Exposing the Secret War against America's Greatest Authors.* New York: D.I. Fine, 1988.

Moffett, James. *Storm in the Mountains: A Case Study of Censorship, Conflict and Consciousness.* Chicago: Southern Illinois University Press, 1988.

Morton, Desmond. "The Wonder of Libraries: Illusion and Reality," in *Focus,* Winter 1986.

New York Public Library. *Censorship: 500 Years of Conflict.* New York: Oxford University Press, 1984.

Newman, Judith M., ed. *Whole Language: Theory in Use.* Portsmouth, N.H.: Heinemann, 1985.

Newsletter on Intellectual Freedom. ALA Intellectual Freedom Committee: Chicago, Ill. Issued six times a year.

Noble, Kimberley. *Climate of Fear: Libel Law and the Failure of Democracy.* Toronto: Harper Collins, 1992.

Oboler, Eli M. *The Fear of the Word: Censorship and Sex.* Metuchen, N.J.: Scarecrow Press, 1974.

Paterson, Katherine. *The Spying Heart.* New York: E.P. Dutton, 1989.

Peck, Richard. "The Great Library-Shelf Witch Hunt," in *Booklist*, January 1, 1992.

People for the American Way. *Attacks on Freedom to Learn.* Washington, D.C.: PFAW (Annual Report).

Rudman, Masha Kabakow. *Children's Literature: An Issues Approach.* New York: Longman, 1978.

Schexnavdre, Linda, and Nancy Burns. *Censorship: A Guide for Successful Workshop Planning.* Phoenix, Ariz.: Onyx Press, 1984.

Schmeiser, D.A. *Civil Liberties in Canada.* London: Oxford University Press, 1964.

Schrader, Alvin. "A Study of Community Censorship Pressures on Canadian Public Libraries," in *Canadian Library Journal*, Vol. 49, No. 1, February 1992.

Schrader, Alvin M., and Keith Walker. "Censorship Iceberg — Alberta," in *Canadian Library Journal*, Vol. 43, No. 2, April 1986.

Simmons, John S. "U.S. Censorship: An Increasing Fact of Life," in *Reading and Response*, edited by Michael Hayhoe and Stephen Parker. Milton Keynes, U.K.: Open University Press, 1990.

Steinhart, Allan L. *Civil Censorship in Canada During World War I.* Toronto: Unitrade Press, 1986.

Sutherland, Zena. *The Best in Children's Books: The University of Chicago Guide to Children's Literature*, 1979-1984. Chicago: University of Chicago Press, 1986.

Theiner, George (ed.). *They Shoot Writers, Don't They.* London: Faber and Faber, 1984.

Toronto Arts Group for Human Rights. *The Writer and Human Rights.* Toronto: Lester & Orpen Dennys, 1983.

Tucker, Nicholas. "Books that Frighten," in *Children and Literature, Views and Reviews*, ed. Virginia Haviland. Glenview, Illinois: Scott Foresman, 1973.

Tucker, Nicholas. *Suitable for Children? Controversies in Children's Literature.* Los Angeles: University of California Press, 1976.

Vivian, Frederick. *Human Freedom and Responsibility.* London: Chatto & Windus, 1964.

West, Mark (ed.) *Trust Your Children: Voices Against Censorship in Children's Literature.* New York: Neal-Schuman Publishers, 1988.

Acknowledgements

I wish to gratefully acknowledge the contributions of so many people who are struggling to bring stories to children:

- the school district members in the U.S. who responded to the *Impressions* struggle with carefully written, well documented reports, particularly in Dixon Unified School District, Yucaipa Joint Unified School District, Lincoln Unified School District, and Oak Harbor School District;

- the teachers in the classrooms of Canada and the United States who made *Impressions* a significant part of their programs;

- the consultants and administrators who continue to believe in their carefully worked out policies and guidelines concerning books for children;

- the parents who care not only about the reading lives of their own children but about the literary and literacy needs of children without advocates;

- the editorial team of *Impressions* who built these magic books: Jack Booth, Jo Phenix, Willa Pauli, and Larry Swartz;

- the editors at HBJ/Holt, all of them, who read critically and responded compassionately;

- the library staff at the Faculty of Education, University of Toronto, for their help in researching this book;

- David Kilgour for editing my feelings into prose;

- Adrian Peetoom, who opens up doors into vistas I would otherwise miss;

- Wendy Cochran, Tom Williamson, Jan Spalding, Cary Lindsay, Bruce Cummings, and Peter Carver for their support under fire.

6038